The Flight
of the Condor

Also by Michael Alford Andrews

The Life that Lives on Man
Year with Three Summers (with R.W. Mackworth Praed)

The Flight
of the Condor
a wildlife exploration of the Andes

Michael Alford Andrews

COLLINS
BRITISH BROADCASTING CORPORATION
1982

For Janet

Author's Note:

Both feet and metres are currently in use in Great Britain but not in the USA. For this book, as far as possible miles have been retained and feet for the height of mountains, whilst metres are used for more precise measurements. 1 metre equals 3.2808 feet.

Scientific names of species not provided in the text can be found in the index.

Published by William Collins Sons and Co Ltd
London, Glasgow, Sydney, Auckland, Toronto, Johannesburg
and the British Broadcasting Corporation
35 Marylebone High Street, London W1M 4AA

First published 1982
© Michael Alford Andrews 1982

ISBN 0-00-219545-3
ISBN 0-563-17991-0

Contents

Introduction

When I was in my teens a schoolfriend was arrowed to death by Indians while exploring in the Amazon rain-forest. This dramatic and tragic event filled me with a sense of the danger and fascination of South America. And as soon as the tiresome business of education allowed I too rolled down to Rio – for those were the days before the jet engine shrank the globe – with a shiny new Land Rover battened in the hold. With three friends from Cambridge University I spent over a year driving from Tierra del Fuego to Alaska. It was, of course, when we got off the road that the adventures began, and soon I was in love with the wildness of the Andes mountains.

We became the first men not born in Tierra del Fuego to cross the mountains to Harberton on the Beagle Channel. Many travellers have commented on the pearly light which shines over these distant channels and mountains, and I was overwhelmed by their beauty. Growing there was the box-leafed barberry, the 'calafate', and they say that if you eat its berries you will always return for more. I picked and ate a handful and they tasted very sweet.

Twenty years passed before I had the opportunity and the experience to turn my love of the Andes into film. I wished to show not just the grandeur and the loneliness of a journey through the mountains, but the wonder of the plant and animal life they cradled. A bird's eye-view, but with the keen eyesight of a hunter. A condor's eye-view.

There were to be three programmes: the first would follow the mountains northwards from Cape Horn past the ice, fiords and forests of Patagonia to the volcanoes and monkey-puzzle forests of southern Chile, and Aconcagua, the highest mountain in the Americas. The second would begin in the teeming tropical waters of the Pacific ocean, would cross the shore to the driest desert in the world, the Atacama, and ascend to the cold bleak highlands dominated by volcanoes and salt flats, the home of the llama and the vicuña. It would then show how those high plateaux became less hostile to life around the basin of the great Lake Titicaca in Peru. The third programme would continue, not northwards, where I would have a repetition of the highland habitats through Colombia and some rather unattractive mangrove swamps on the Caribbean, but sideways: a trace from west to east, from the high volcanoes like Cotopaxi on the equator down into the Amazon jungle. Although many films have been made about the Amazon, nobody had made a detailed film about the changing wildlife found from the icy highland world of the condor down to the flooded forest of the anaconda.

In the south the Andes lie mostly within Chile. I would like to have filmed in Bolivia, but three changes of government in a year deterred me. So we filmed mostly in Chile, Peru, and Ecuador. The lower Amazon of Brazil was another story for another time. I organised five main filming trips according to the best seasons for filming animal life in each area, but in this account they have been simplified into a progression from south to north, as in the films.

My role was to organise, so that highly skilled professional wildlife cameramen could have the best chance of filming the animals, and our combined efforts depended greatly on the information and practical help I was given by local and foreign scientists and naturalists. Without them a task, already difficult, would have been well-nigh impossible, for South America, biologically speaking, is still the unknown continent.

Film-making is a team effort, and a list of those to whom the credit is due for any success the series may achieve appears at the end of the book. But all of them would agree that we owe a debt to my right-hand man Donaldo MacIver, the only member of the team who went with me on all the filming trips. His steadfastness and humour carried us through some black moments.

I had met him first in Buenos Aires. I thought he looked a little distracted when he arrived at my hotel, and I was surprised when he declined lunch. It was only months later that he told me that as he got out of his taxi to meet me shots had been fired. He threw himself to the gutter and a man was shot dead only a few feet away.

But this book is not just about our adventures making the series, though there were many. Nor is it simply a recompilation of the scripts: that would occupy only one chapter. Instead it is intended to be complementary to the films: a more detailed background to the stunning film that the cameramen achieved – an account of the story of the Andes and its wildlife as witnessed by us, and the experience of being amongst the mountains in some of the least-known wilderness in the world.

Maps

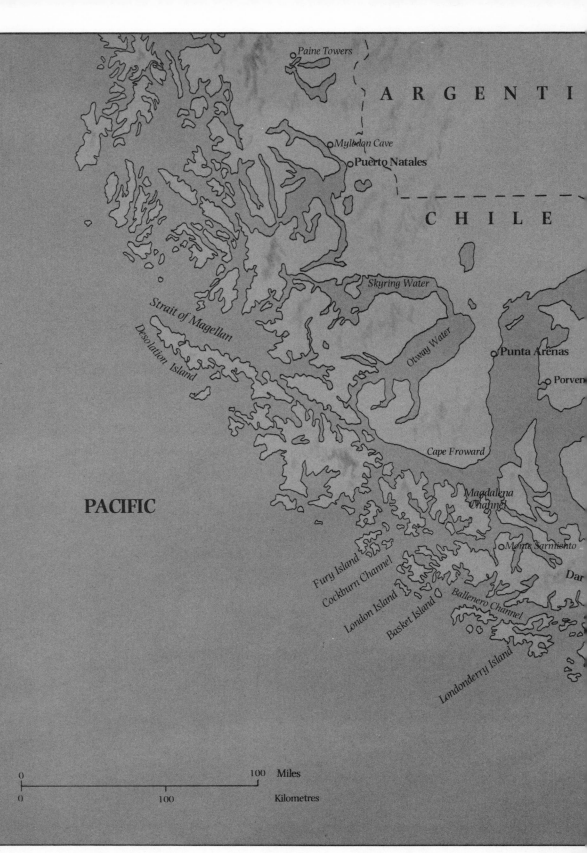

Paine Towers

ARGENTI

Mylodan Cave
Puerto Natales

CHILE

Skyring Water

Strait of Magellan

Desolation Island

Otway Water

Punta Arenas

Porven

Cape Froward

PACIFIC

Magdalena
Channel

Monte Sarmiento

Dar

Fury Island

Cockburn Channel

London Island

Basket Island

Ballenero Channel

Londonderry Island

0   100   Miles
0   100   Kilometres

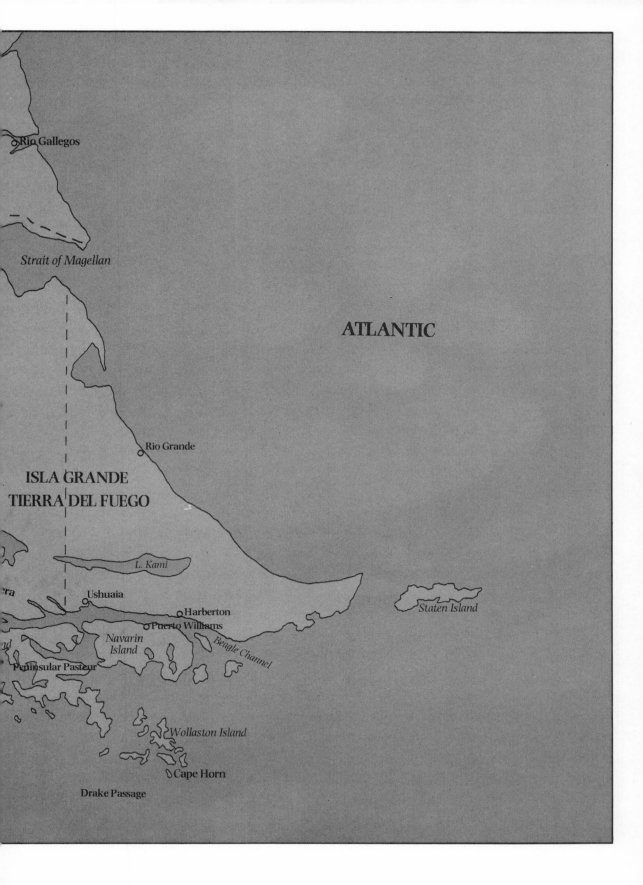

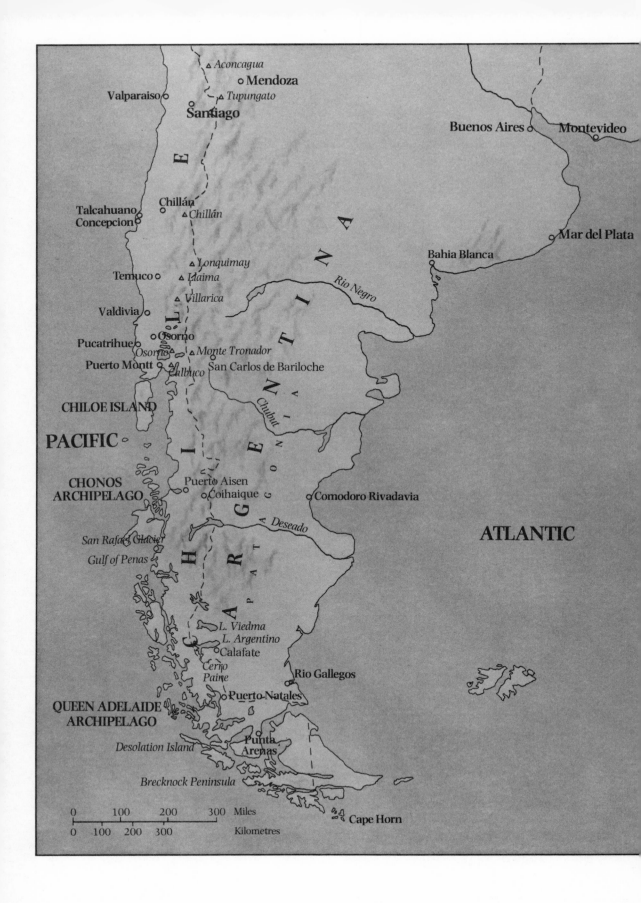

△ *Aconcagua*
● **Mendoza**
Valparaiso ○
△ *Tupungato*
Santiago

Buenos Aires ○ ● **Montevideo**

● **Mar del Plata**

Chillán
Talcahuano
Concepcion ○
△ *Chillán*

Bahia Blanca

Rio Negro

△ *Lonquimay*
Temuco ○ △ *Llaima*

△ *Villarica*
Valdivia ○
Pucatrihue ○ ○ **Osorno**
○ *Osorno* △ *Monte Tronador*
Puerto Montt ○ ○ *Calbuco*
San Carlos de Bariloche

A R G E N T I N A

Chubut

CHILOE ISLAND

PACIFIC

CHONOS
ARCHIPELAGO
Puerto Aisen ○
○ Coihaique
○ **Comodoro Rivadavia**

ATLANTIC

Deseado

San Rafael Glacier
Gulf of Penas

C H I L E

P A T A G O N I A

L. Viedma
L. Argentino
○ **Calafate**
Cerro
Paine
Rio Gallegos
○ **Puerto Natales**

QUEEN ADELAIDE
ARCHIPELAGO

Desolation Island
Punta
Arenas

Brecknock Peninsula

0   100   200   300   Miles
0   100   200   300
Kilometres

Cape Horn

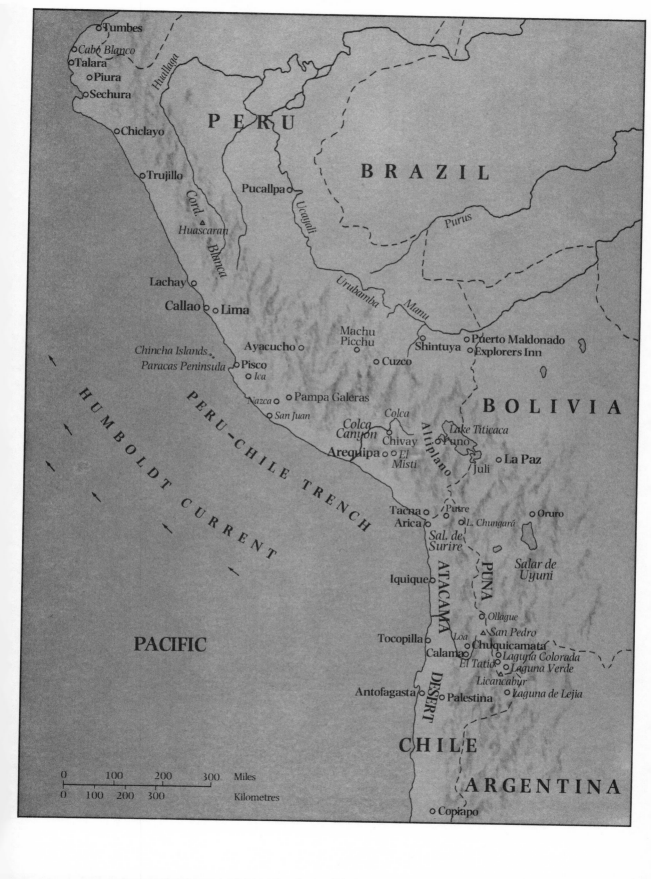

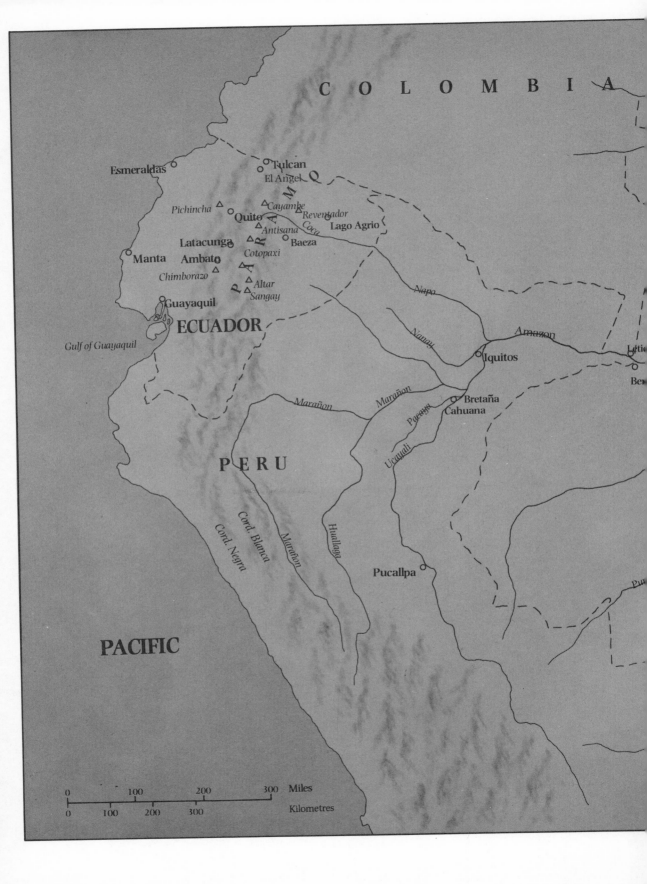

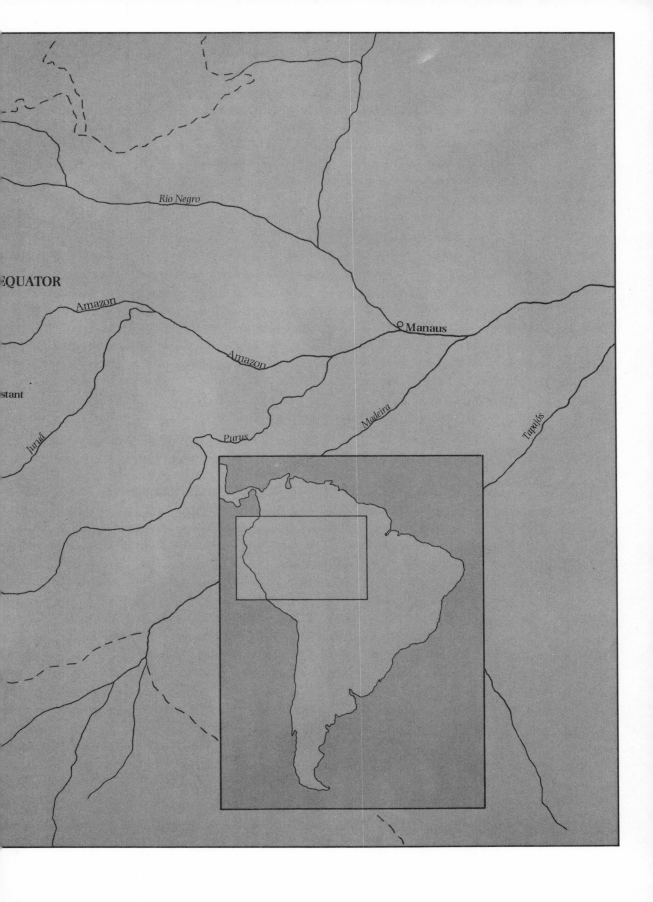

1

The Islands of Tierra del Fuego and Cape Horn

Curving down the western edge of the continent of South America lies the greatest mountain chain in the world: the Cordillera of the Andes. Four thousand three hundred miles long, it stretches in an uninterrupted line from the Caribbean to Cape Horn. The Himalayas may have higher peaks and a greater breadth, but they cannot compete in length. No other continent possesses a north-south range which cuts straight through the tropics, bringing glaciers to the equator; no other range forms such a barrier dividing climate and species. It is as if a chain of massive peaks ran from southern Scotland to Angola without a break.

South America has twice the area of land over 5000 feet high as Africa, and great capital cities such as Bogotá, Quito, and La Paz are set at heights that would be unthinkable elsewhere. In the centre the Cordillera is 500 miles wide, and contains the highest navigable lake in the world, a great inland sea nestling more than two miles above sea level: Lake Titicaca. In the north an avenue of great snow-capped volcanoes strides across the equator. In the south the snow-line drops to 2000 feet and huge glaciers descend from ice-caps to calve directly into the sea.

The Andes are not just the greatest, they are also the youngest mountain chain. Scarcely a year goes by without a major earthquake somewhere along their length, and hundreds of active volcanoes smoke and rumble in the rarefied air. They form part of the circle of volcanoes, the 'Ring of Fire' that surrounds the Pacific Ocean, where the earth's crust sinks beneath the continents.

The diversity of wildlife in a continent depends on its geological history and the variety of its habitats. South America has an unparalleled range of habitats, from the immense rain forest of the Amazon Basin, to the Atacama Desert – far dryer than the dead heart of Australia or the Sahara. Its history, too, is complicated, and considering its area, it has by far the richest animal population of any continent.

South America, there is now no doubt, was once joined to Africa. When it drifted away and the Atlantic opened up, it was for a long time connected to Antarctica. In ensuing ages, the tips of South America and Antarctica were left stretched like a piece of toffee towards the east, towards the Scotia Arc of South Georgia, the South Sandwich Islands and the South Orkneys. Although there is still volcanic activity in Tierra del Fuego, it is on a minor scale, and the mountains have been planed down by the ice, which was once 10,000 feet thick, to comparatively low altitudes. Not all of them however; the peaks of the Darwin Cordillera, the last outposts of the Andes, reach 8200 feet. The whole area is so little known that the highest mountain was only identified by Eric Shipton in 1962. Beyond the main navigable channels, hundreds of islands are uncharted, and as we flew low over the chaos of sea and land, I knew that many of the hidden corrie lakes which we filmed had never been seen before. The canoe-Indians did not venture far ashore, and the weather is usually so appalling that a flight like ours was quite exceptional.

On the western edge of the archipelago over five metres (200 inches) of rain fall in the year, and the rock that was not destroyed by the last ice-age has been bombarded ever since by the force of the westerly gales until it is the most fragmented coastline in the world. The Isla Grande, the 'mainland' of Tierra del Fuego, lies to the north-east, and there the major forests, and in the north the grasslands, provided shelter and hunting grounds for the Ona Indians.

To film a representative selection of scenery and animal life from the region I had, of course, to reach Cape Horn. We had filmed it from the air, but I needed close-ups of the animals and vegetation. This meant travelling with the Chilean naval supply ship *Elicura* down through the tortuous channels that lead out almost into the southern Pacific before turning east beneath the Isla Grande. We left Punta Arenas on the Magellan Straits in the evening, and when I awoke we were heading due south down the Magdalena Channel. To port, 7600 feet above us, shone the ice-clad spire of Monte Sarmiento. Magellan had heard the thunder of those curving glaciers as they calved on the ebb tide and had fancied he heard the sound of the surf of the southern ocean booming on the tip of the Americas. So, he maintained, the high mountains to the south were no more than an island – he called the region Tierra del Fuego, from the smoke of the signal fires which heralded his passage.

To starboard a thin fringe of beech forest straggled up from the shore and clung to the sides of a steep valley: the snug cove where Joshua Slocum, the first man to sail alone round the world, had anchored the *Spray*. For four days he had been driven back south by a gale and the last fearsome night he had spent beating to and fro in a huge sea in the midst of the myriad rocks of the Furies that so whiten the sea with broken water that sailors called it the Milky Way.

Finally at anchor, he must have been sleeping like the dead when a party of Indians stole aboard. But Slocum was ready for them. He had scattered his decks with carpet-tacks. 'Worth more than all the fighting men and dogs of Tierra del Fuego.' That was only ninety years ago.

We turned south-west retracing his course towards the most rugged and the most feared coast in the world. Ahead lay Fury Island, and its 100-knot squalls.

In the latitude of Cape Horn the wind and the seas can sweep around and around the globe unhindered by land, the bottom shelves up abruptly from 2000 fathoms to fifty and it is not uncommon for the westerlies to bring in five depressions in two days. Towards the end of the last century eight or nine ships were wrecked every year off Staten Island alone. For once, however, the sky was blue, the sea sparkled like the Mediterranean, and the only breeze came from the motion of the ship. A long long slow swell came up between the cliffs to meet us, the faint echo of a great storm to the south-west. A black-browed albatross strained to take the air. Head down, long blade-like wings flapping heavily, feet flailing the surface, it denied the myth that they can't take off without waves and wind. Once airborne, weightless and graceful as a ballet-dancer, it curved away, skimming the surface with a wingtip, drawing a line in the reflections of the snowy peaks as if with pleasure.

Steam was rising from the damp decks as the sun warmed them. A Magellanic penguin surfaced nearby, looked in alarm at our vessel and dived again. To the south now lay the Brecknock peninsular, the frayed remnant of Tierra del Fuego that stretches out towards what Magellan called – un-believably – the Pacific. The rock shore that rose abruptly from the water was blasted as bare and grey and crinkled as the hide of an elephant. Only the most-sheltered eastern slopes nourished a faint bloom of growth, of moor and bog and golden grass, with thickets of stunted trees bowed and broken to the shape of the sheltering contours. There was a sprinkling of snow on the tops of the hills nearby which hid the peaks of the Darwin Cordillera.

From time to time, now, we passed a patch of green scurvy-grass by a scrap of shore, which grew over the mussel-shell heaps of former Yahgan Indian encampments. But beyond that there was no trace of Man; nothing to challenge the sovereignty of rock, wind and water.

Some time during the 10,000 years or so of Man's wanderings in South America the Yahgan Indians had been squeezed south by other fiercer tribes to people this uttermost part of the earth. The bleak land supports few animals, yet the waters are amongst the richest in the world. The giant kelp which clings to every rock, even on the most gale-dashed coasts, offers shelter between its roots for a multitude of small fish and other species. The channels are rich in krill, and the fish, southern sea-lions, dolphins, whales and seabirds that thrive on this plenty sustained several thousand Yahgan families. They clung to sheltered water and the few tiny coves, and only ventured to the forest to cut the evergreen southern beech for bark for their canoes.

Here was Basket Island; more bare rock hunched against the elements. Here in a storm at four o'clock one foul morning a party of seamen from HMS *Beagle* had had their boat stolen by Indians. From small branches, canvas, and clay they built a basket-like boat which they paddled fifteen miles across rough water before regaining their ship. Later they took as hostage for the return of the whale-boat an Indian girl they called Fuegia Basket. Captain FitzRoy took her to England. It was the need for her return which led to Darwin's visiting South America, and the observations that led to his obsession with evolution.

There are no human voices now to echo between the cliffs where the

Yahgans would catch cormorants on the darkest nights, and while the wildlife that they hunted flourishes, there is an unutterable loneliness about the scene. The columns of smoke from their fires, which gave this mosaic of land and water its romantic name, were quenched by the measles, of all things, and are now replaced in the northern plains by the flames of natural gas flares, appropriate symbols for a more greedy society.

When FitzRoy surveyed the Beagle Channel it was packed with icebergs fallen from the many glaciers in the north-west arm. But the ice-caps are in retreat, the glaciers have crept back up their fiords leaving a scar of bare rock beneath their snouts. We sailed beneath them in the first light of dawn. Blue crevasses glimmered through the mists and beech stood black against the frozen rim which crumbled and thundered hundreds of feet to the water's edge. Eric Shipton was the first man to venture on that vast ice-cap, seen dimly now through the thin cloud. He marvelled that so large an area should still be completely virgin territory, unexplored as late as 1962. Like others before him he learned to respect the wind. It blew away a fifty-pound pack, and hurled a large piece of granite at one of the members of his team.

In an increasingly comfortable and prosperous world the reputation of Cape Horn brings a steady stream of adventurers to the office of the Chilean naval base commander at Puerto Williams. We were yet another group asking for help from his limited fleet. With much forbearance he lent us a tiny converted fishing boat, the *Castor*, under the command of Lieutenant Castro, an enthusiastic young man who was overjoyed at the prospect. We were admonished to be back in four days. It seemed to me a desperately short time and a very small boat in which to make the 250-mile trip to Cape Horn.

My only companion was Hugh Miles, an extremely expert specialist wildlife cameraman, and as we motored down the east side of Navarin Island and into Drake Passage we bunked down on the floor under the table of the tiny dining-room beneath the bridge.

We rolled a good bit in the night and my stomach was none too steady when I went up on the tiny bridge at five the next morning. Our amazing luck with the weather had held. We were now passing between Wollaston and Freycinet Islands and the sun was about to come up in a clear sky. To the south against a sparkling horizon, I could see the shores of Herschel Island of the Hermite group, one of the loneliest places in the world. Beyond it lay Cape Horn. Lieutenant Castro pushed another cassette into his player: it was 'In the Navy' by the Village People. Even here we were part of the electronic village.

Beneath the claw of South America the climate is not quite as wet as further west. In the Cockburn Channel, past Fury Island, one can expect only one day in a hundred of 'calm, sunshine and only occasional rain and snow.' Cape Horn is drier and more sheltered, at least from the north-westerly gales, and vegetation covers most of the island. I wanted to take a good look at it before we landed as it would be difficult to walk with equipment over the tussock-grass. Lieutenant Castro had never taken his ship round the Horn, but seeing that the sea was flat calm, he took little persuasion. Soon we were sailing from the Atlantic to the Pacific.

The name Cape Horn has nothing to do with the shape of the dark cliff that rose above us. In 1616 Willem Schouten named it after his native village Hoorn. But the name is not unfitting for the broken headland where the Andes finally give up their struggle to rise above the sea. Crowned with jagged pinnacles, it dramatises the break with the ice-polished curves of the islands behind.

At its base a slow swell foamed amongst the rocks. On one of these it's said that Sir Francis Drake lay on his chest with his head and shoulders over the sea and boasted delightedly that he had been further south on land than any other man. Others maintain that he muddied his doublet on the Diego Ramirez Islands thirty-five miles further south and that he never even saw Cape Horn.

We chugged slowly round the island and then landed in a whaler on a boulder beach on the south-east corner. If rounding the Horn had been an anti-climax, landing on it was even more so. We were met by a Chilean army sergeant with a platoon of men who helped us carry the filming gear up a steep slope of dwarfed beech-trees and through the tussock-grass to their hut. It was seven in the morning when we got there and the floor of the hut was full of Frenchmen in sleeping-bags. They were playing at rounding the Horn on wind-surf boats, but in fact were using commando-type high-powered inflatables.

Hugh and I set off on a rapid reconnaissance of the nearby shore and hillsides where Magellanic penguins were striving to keep a nesting colony going against the opposition of the soldiers' dogs, which killed three birds while we were there.

On top of the cliffs of the windward edge of the island even tussock-grass could not survive and was burnt brown. But below, gentle waves washed to and fro in channels between the rocks, to which clung the tresses of giant kelp, visible in the clear water. It was astonishing that it could survive the pounding of the gales. This slippery tubular seaweed, about an inch in diameter, can grow to the length of 300 feet from a depth of 150 feet, though in these turbulent seas it was much shorter. The stems are a honeycomb of air bladders and the tough floating masses which fringe the shores form surprisingly efficient breakwaters. In places where the Yahgan Indians could not beach their canoes the women would moor them to the kelp. They would then swim to the shore with ice forming in their hair. This sex discrimination was sound medically: women possess an insulating layer of subcutaneous fat that men do not, and are more resistant to cold.

In the pale sunshine, an arctic tern was patrolling the kelp, diving for small fish. It was unbelievable that this sleek bundle of feathers should fly the length of two American continents twice a year. With all the plenty of the Pacific coast that it must pass on the way it seemed so pointless too, yet the presence of this white, dancing figure countered the disappointment of finding the island full of people.

One of the greatest problems of filming wildlife in an area as remote as Tierra del Fuego is that it is impossible to get accurate information. It is also impossible to go there twice on account of the cost. So when we arrived on Cape Horn I was far from certain what we would be filming. Indeed I had been told that chinstrap penguins, an Antarctic species, were nesting on Cape Horn, a report we now discovered to be false. Rockhopper penguins, on the other hand, although common on Staten Island, only nest on one or two of the remotest rocks of the archipelago of Tierra del Fuego, so when I discovered that there was a colony on a rock south of the Cape it was a stroke of luck, especially since rockhoppers are usually fearless and could probably be approached closely.

When, months later, we looked at the film, we found that there were not only rockhopper penguins with their chicks, but breeding pairs of Macaroni penguins, an Antarctic species seldom recorded in South America. This was not the last surprise we were to have about the animals of this continent, which has been studied so little.

We anchored that night in Scourfield Bay on Wollaston Island, a good landlocked anchorage, and a spot as remote and beautiful as Cape Horn should have been. It was the first time I had landed on an uninhabited island, and it was an exciting prospect. The only way we could find through the thicket of matted dwarf trees that fringed the boulder beach was to follow up a stream that ran in a tunnel of vegetation. We then scrambled over bog and tussock for three quarters of an hour, floundering, as one minute we would disappear to our waists and the next have to step as high as our chins. At last we reached a still, silent corrie lake hidden in a circle of cliffs dusted with snow. Edible berries gleamed in the moss at our feet and the water tasted soft and peaty. There was not a sign of animal or human, and I wondered who, if anyone, had last seen it.

In 1832 HMS *Beagle* had dropped anchor at Wollaston Island, probably in the self-same cove. Charles Darwin wrote in his journal that they pulled alongside a canoe with six Fuegians. 'These were the most abject and miserable creatures I anywhere beheld . . . quite naked, and even one fully grown woman was absolutely so. It was raining heavily, and the fresh water together with the spray, tricked down her body. In another harbour not far distant, a woman, who was suckling a recently-born child, came one day alongside the vessel, and remained there out of mere curiosity, whilst the sleet fell and thawed on her naked bosom and on the skin of her naked baby! These poor wretches were stunted in their growth, their hideous faces bedaubed with white paint, their skins filthy and greasy, their hair entangled, their voices discordant, and their gestures violent. Viewing such men, one can hardly make oneself believe that they are fellow-creatures and inhabitants of the same world.'

These 'wretched natives', the southernmost inhabitants of the planet, were found to have a vocabulary of more than 32,000 words which described their environment and life in a far more precise manner than could be done in English.

In the little museum on Navarin Island I bought a beautiful reed basket plaited by a ninety-year-old woman who is one of the last surviving pure-blooded Yamana, as the Yahgans are now called. At first I wanted to go to see her, but what can you say to a woman who has outlived her tribe by almost a hundred years? Even the name she answered to – Rosa Miliciç – belonged to two separate invading cultures. Her Yahgan name was Leukutaia Lekipa.

In the morning rain was driving in from the west, but in a lull Hugh and I got our boat launched to try to film some of the wind-blown vegetation. As we cruised past a cliff, Hugh spotted what appeared to be a dead duck lying on a rock in a crumpled-looking position with its head outstretched towards the water. We guessed that it might be a flightless steamer duck shamming, and sure enough, before we had a chance to get it lined up to film, it slipped quietly into the water, to reappear about eighty yards behind us.

Steamer ducks are a genus confined to the cold extremity of South America and the Falkland Islands. There is much disagreement about how many species of steamer duck there may be, but south of Isla Grande it appeared to us that one species can fly, and another has stunted wings and cannot. Early observers made the mistake of thinking that they were the same bird and that it was older, heavier birds – which are said to weigh more than twenty pounds – which were unable to fly. The Indians made no such mistake, and called them by different names. We found the two fairly easy to distinguish because the flightless variety has a light-coloured stripe behind the eye.

A flightless steamer duck will rush away across the surface of the water when disturbed, paddling with its feet and flailing the surface with its stumpy wings, making a ludicrous commotion and a good deal of spray – thus earning its name from sailors contemptuous of paddle-steamers. We found that they could 'steam' at ten knots at least, and if further pressed they would dive. It was believed that they beat their wings alternately. Darwin reported this, and it is repeated as fact in Johnson's *Birds of Chile*. It is reminiscent of the old country belief that swifts beat their wings alternately, a myth only disproved by the cine-camera. Having now had the opportunity to analyse our own film of the ducks I can say categorically that they beat their wings simultaneously.

They are common birds throughout the archipelago of Tierra del Fuego. We watched them apparently defending feeding territories in kelp beds off Navarin Island, and filmed them coming ashore to drink at a stream that ran across a shingle beach. They are still hunted for their tasty flesh and we found them hard to approach. It is interesting to speculate why they are flightless; it could be because there are few predators in the wild area where they live, or even that in this region of thick weather and gales it is actually a difficult and dangerous place to fly. It is more probable that small wings enable them to dive better for the shellfish on which they feed.

Another engaging bird confined to the region is the kelp goose. It is absolutely unmistakeable from a distance as the male appears completely white and the female black. They are found in solitary pairs throughout the islands and channels, nearly always by the shoreline, and they get their name from their diet of seaweed. (We invariably saw them grazing on the green sea-lettuce *Ulva* and not the 'luche' red algae which others have claimed to be their diet.) Their rather absurdly short legs and large yellow webbed feet help them to perch on the slippery tidal rocks where we saw them so often, and allow them to bend down to graze the seaweed growing beneath their feet.

Rain soon drove us back aboard again, and we set off north-west up Nassau Bay. Here our small ship began to roll, making it difficult for Hugh who was trying to film albatrosses. As well as black-brows we saw the dark giant fulmar or petrel, a fierce scavenger and bird of prey whose unpleasant habits of feeding off carrion at seal colonies earned it the name of the Stinker. Powerful birds, they circle the globe around the entire southern ocean and reach as far north as the tropics.

We were now passing close to a large bay named on both Admiralty and Chilean charts as Bahia Tekenika. This is close to one of the areas settled by the Yahgan Indians, and the name has been adopted for gift shops and various touristic purposes. It is an absurd name. The word in the Yahgan tongue means 'difficult' or 'awkward to see or understand.' No doubt the bay was pointed out to a native who, when asked the name of it, answered 'Teke uneka', implying 'I don't understand what you mean', and down went the name 'Tekenika.' Such misunderstandings are not uncommon, but for me it exemplified both the white man's failure to understand the Indian, and his rush to cash in on the memory of what he had destroyed.

I had been anxious to land on one of the islands of the inner channels, all of which are uninhabited except for widely separated military posts, to film in the wet windblown forest, which does not grow on Cape Horn. Canal Canacos was suggested. It did not appear on my chart, but on the large-scale Chilean one it showed up between Milne Edwards island and the Pasteur Peninsula. Lieutenant Castro was at first adamant that his ship could not enter the narrow passage, but after consultation agreed to have a go. We slipped through a tight channel into a series of coves surrounded by tall nothofagus beech trees. We anchored and stopped the engine and in the pool of silence I could hear the trilling of an Austral thrush from the woods and the piping of oyster-catchers. I ferried the sailors ashore in our dinghy to hunt for mussels, and Hugh and I went off to film. It was a most beautiful place.

We landed on an islet where the wind had cut the stunted trees to a sculpted curve as neatly as any gardener. Almost at once I found a Magellanic oyster-catcher's nest. Three dark mottled eggs lay in a scrape decorated with pearly mussel shells surrounded by sea-pinks. It was the prettiest nest I had ever seen. The adults' plaintive call at any hour of the day or night makes them the watch-dog of the channels and their neat black-and-white plumage was reflected in the shallows as they fluttered, piping, from rock to rock trying to draw us away from the nest.

Then I almost trod on the nest of a flightless steamer-duck. I had seen the female emerge from the bushes as we landed, but the nests are notoriously difficult to find as they are usually hidden deep in the impenetrable thickets. But this island was full of nests, most of them still being incubated, each with five to eight very large ivory-coloured eggs.

The sun was now bursting through a magnificent roll of black clouds to the west over Hoste Island and we paddled across the calm water of the bay, filming the beds of kelp lying in the water. Then we landed to film the fungus *Cyttaria darwinii* that grows like orange squash-balls clinging to the trunk of the beech trees, whose small green leaves were shining in the slanting light. This was another important source of food for the Indians, who collected the fungus and dried it on sticks for food in the winter. I was interested to see that our sailors had collected it too. It had a tasteless, spongy texture and certainly was no delicacy.

Hugh was filming the stark outlines of the dead beech trees crooked against the snow and sky and raging clouds, or lying on the pearly mussel shells where they had fallen generations before. They are a good indication of the climate – so cold that even bacteria do not flourish and things rot slowly. I wandered along the lonely shore, listening to the voices of the geese and oyster-catchers, watching the clear water lap on the rocks and the snow squalls shrouding the distant mountains. A rainbow curved through the forest and the light reflected from the water on the underside of the trees. The place had a purity, a spirit, a mood all its own, and I felt that it was urging me to stay. I felt that I knew no other place in the world that was more beautiful.

Darwin, though impressed by the 'savage magnificence' of Tierra del Fuego, found it desolate, sombre and gloomy: 'as appearing to lead to another and worse world'. To someone who was continually seasick, and who had had to beat to windward in gales for weeks to attain the shelter of the islands, it is surprising that these shores did not seem more friendly. The gales, the uncharted waters, and the williwaws (unheralded squalls – 'compressed gales of wind handed down over the hills in chunks') make it a fearful place to navigate under sail and Darwin's only company was that of seamen. The amazing surveys of this coast by Sarmiento, Stokes, FitzRoy, Skyring, and others, were amost all conducted from open boats under oars, because it was impossible to make to windward in the channels in square-riggers, a problem which still confronts yachtsmen even with today's far more sophisticated rigs. A good williwaw will tip a sailing boat on her beam-ends even when she is carrying no sail. Magnetic anomalies affect the compass, and deep water and kelp make for bad holding ground, so that many a ship has been lost through dragging her anchors.

A century ago the seamen that wrote of these islands were from cultures which strove to dominate not just nations but Nature herself. An untamed landscape was an adversary or a challenge or fit for nothing. The names on the charts reflect their views: Desolation Island, Useless Bay, Famine Reach. . . . Pioneers cannot afford to be tolerant. Land was to be ploughed, forests burnt, rivers bridged, swamps drained, imported plants, animals and ideals cultivated.

The flood tide of that logic has now left even the shores of the Beagle Channel littered with red plastic carrier-bags printed with penguins, and Argentine deodorant bottles. But in the outer islands one can still step ashore without putting a foot on a broken bottle. Here remains something rare and wonderful and seldom witnessed today – unspoilt creation.

Back on the deck of the *Castor* the sailors were shelling the mussels. The deep-water mussel known locally as the cholga grows to a large size. Drake reported finding them twenty inches long, though it's rare to find them half that length now. We sat on the deck eating them straight from the sea with *Cyttaria* fungus as bread. They were delicious, and this time even the fungus tasted good.

Working with Hugh Miles was an education; he was brilliant at spotting the small detail of an animal's behaviour that would make all the difference to our chances of filming it doing something interesting. He seemed to think like the animal he was stalking. It is, after all, far harder to get good film of an animal than to shoot it, the most important difference being that the animal must not be aware – or must not show that it is aware – of being filmed, or the whole film looks artificial. The north shore of Navarin Island proved a good place to film the bird-life of the Beagle Channel. We would drive along the track skirting the shore and stop at each corner to observe the bay below through binoculars before planning what to do. Sometimes Hugh would use a hide, and would direct me by radio how to work the birds his way; at other times we would use the cover of the big circular piles of shells that had once ringed Yahgan wigwams.

The most common bird was the upland goose, and one day I saw a curious incident. A family with six small goslings was swimming through a bed of kelp with the female in the lead and the gander bringing up the rear. Suddenly another gander flew in and attacked the rearguard. There was a tremendous fight with spray flying, and then the female rushed away, calling loudly, with only five goslings. Her mate soon fled after her, honking, and the attacking male was left with one gosling which it attacked furiously, stabbing at it with its beak as it bobbed on the water. It repeatedly picked up the unfortunate ball of down, shaking it by the neck and finally thrusting it below the water several times before swallowing it whole with much subsequent gaping and neck-stretching. All the time the female and male of the brood were swimming off with their diminished family making frenzied alarm calls, the gander having made no attempt to save its young.

I was quite shocked, not just that a grass-eating goose should turn cannibal, but at the revelation of the violence latent in this country of extremes.

2

The Magellan Straits
and North to Patagonia

With the map of South America banished to the last page of the atlas, it is difficult to comprehend the scale of the battleground between the Andes mountains and the elements – the mad mosaic of islands and channels that fringe the Pacific coast where the continent points towards Antarctica and sinks beneath the sea. But look at a globe and some comparisons emerge.

Cape Horn is roughly at the latitude of the river Clyde. Turn South America on its head, with Cape Horn at Glasgow, and the archipelago would stretch to the north-west corner of Spain in a band between sixty and a hundred and fifty miles wide. Tierra del Fuego with its associated islands would spread out over an area roughly equal in latitude and size to Ireland. The mainland of South America would begin at Dublin. But the more this analogy is applied, the less it seems to fit. On this basis a glacier rising in the Tyrol would cast icebergs into the Mediterranean at Venice and the aeronautical and Admiralty charts of Europe would be full of warnings and blanks.

The difference, of course, is the climate, and that blue sash of ocean which girdles the globe from latitude 56° south which allows the depressions and the storms free scope to rage unchecked by land. Where the Andes intrude into this dominion of the wind they drag incredible quantities of water from the sky. On Desolation Island, where the Magellan Straits join the Pacific, five metres of rain fall in a year, making it one of the wettest places on earth. Yet 120 miles to the east, on the other side of the Andes, only half a metre falls.

The British are brought up to believe that their climate is abnormal, but for all our bones may tell us to the contrary, it is about 5° Celsius warmer than it should be if latitude alone were to rule. That does not sound much, but 5° are enough to keep the glaciers off Dartmoor. We owe this warmth to the obliging Gulf Stream. Without it Britain would be as bleak as Tierra del Fuego.

The Magellan Strait does not run east–west but in a broad 'V' round the southernmost headland of South America, Cape Froward. To the north-west of Cape Froward the islands are clothed with stunted beech forest so cold that the fallen trees do not rot, but lie in piles hundreds of years deep. To the north-east the Andes soon give way to a great plain of gravel, sand, and mud which stretches to the Atlantic. This is the debris chiselled from the mountains by ice, polished by water, and blown by the wind over sixty-five million years. The Patagonian Steppe is a cold land of scrub and alkaline lagoons dominated by the wind, which, having shed its moisture on the islands, so desiccates the land that it creates a semi-desert reaching as far north as the Rio Negro.

Clipper ships preferred to give the Horn a wide berth to avoid the uncharted rocks of the long lee shore in the thick weather which prevails so much of the time. But during the age of coal-fired steam and Californian gold, before the opening of the Panama Canal, a town prospered briefly beside a good anchorage on the mainland shore.

Punta Arenas still has strategic importance; it still exports wool and frozen lamb and tinned crab; offshore oil rigs and the armed forces keep the money flowing. But it is a town that reeks of the past, and is dominated by the wind. When I first went there, people were hanging onto the lamp-posts so as not to be blown off their feet, and the big American cars, spoils of a free port, were bobbing up and down on their springs while parked at the kerb like dinghies anchored in a choppy sea. I could not go out without getting my eyes full of grit – and the locals say that if you want to see Patagonia all you have to do is stand still and it will blow past you. This time it was calm.

Flying down from Santiago I noticed that as we approached the south the entire Andes were visible from the plane, ideal for filming, so I drove straight to the Catalina airforce base where I told a rather surprised-looking guard that I wanted him to ring the General at home because I needed a plane. It was Saturday, and they had only a skeleton staff on duty, but within two hours we were airborne again in a twenty-seat Twin Otter of the Chilean Airforce. While the air-crew drove in we had had the door taken off so that we could film the glaciers of the southern ice-cap. It was going to be a cold flight.

We flew north for an hour to the Paine massif (pronounced Piney). It was nearly eight o'clock in the evening when we reached the glaciers and spires of this superb range, but in the long evening of these high latitudes there was still plenty of daylight and the shadows lay stretched blue across the moulded contours of the ice. For an hour we flew round and over and beneath the jagged fingers of granite that form the Paine Towers. By degrees I persuaded the pilot to fly closer and closer until the wingtip was almost brushing the snow from the peaks. Some had huge cornices of snow compacted by the gales and with the red rock that the wind had stripped bare they reminded me of enormous cream-topped cakes. We had the amazing good fortune to have completely still air. It was like going along on wheels, ideal for filming. We felt well satisfied when we touched down in the dark at Punta Arenas.

When Magellan first entered the strait that bears his name he stopped at 'two islands full of geese and seawolves', according to his chronicler Antonio Pigafetta. 'Truly the great number of these geese cannot be reckoned,' he noted. 'In one hour we loaded the five ships with them. Those geese are black and have

all their feathers alike, both on body and wings. They do not fly and live on fish.'
We now call them Magellanic penguins.

It gives some idea of the scarcity of fresh food on these early voyages that
Drake should have revictualled in the same place. His sailors killed 3000
penguins in one day and wrote that their 'flesh is not unlike fat goose here in
England.' A tradition grew up of exploiting the huge colonies of birds and sealions, which led to millions of penguins being boiled for their oil, and almost led to
the extinction of the southern sealions. This depredation continues today with
fishermen using penguins as bait for the crab pots to trap the huge and delicious
centolla or southern king crab – itself in danger from over-fishing.

It was the fishing season and every available boat was out crabbing. That
was bad news both for the penguins and for us, as we found it very difficult to
find a boat to take us to Magdalena island, very probably one of the islands that
Magellan and Drake had plundered, now a national reserve.

Although most people associate penguins with the ice of the Antarctic they
have a very wide distribution along the shores of South America. Later in our
journeying it was strange to see Humboldt penguins nesting beneath cactus
plants on the shores of the Atacama Desert, and there is a separate species on
the Galapagos Islands.

It was raining gently as we set up camp on the island with our new tents.
Choosing those tents had given me some anxiety in England. Would they stand
up to the Patagonian wind? I need not have worried. The strait was calm and in
five weeks of filming we never had a gale. Dependent as we were on fine
weather, we could not believe our luck.

From the door of my tent I could see the low blue strip of the coast of Isla
Grande, Tierra del Fuego. The straits were a lighter blue and across the short
cropped grass of the foreground waddled the penguins to their burrows.
Penguins are amongst the most popular animals and there is something
irredeemably comic about them. Their sober black dress and lurching gait,
'arms' akimbo, reminds one of a drunken funeral procession. It was early in the
nesting season and most pairs were sitting on two eggs. About every two hours
the parents relieve each other at the nest so there was a regular coming and
going to the sea along well-defined penguin highways which wound down the
soft sedimentary cliffs to the sea. At first all that could be seen were a few groups
gathered hesitantly at the edge of the surf and a sparse honeycomb of oval
burrows. But as we approached an angry head appeared in each burrow, not
only wagging from side to side but corkscrewing round almost through 360
degrees in a most ludicrous fashion. We estimated that there were about 2000
birds there and the smell was as impressive as the noise.

They are also called jackass penguins, and well they merit it. That night as
we lay in our tents, with some nests only a metre away, the colony first
entertained and then appalled us with a hideous crescendo of braying like a
cross between a hiccoughing donkey and someone stamping rhythmically on
an accordion.

When we landed we had been concerned to see that in one bay of the island, which is about two-thirds of a mile long, there was an encampment of fishermen. We knew that our outboard would be a valued prize for them and had taken the precaution of carrying it up to the camp and tying it on to the guy-ropes of Hugh's tent. In the middle of the night he woke and immediately sat bolt upright. Somebody was pulling at the guy-rope. Cautiously he moved to the tent flap, to be confronted not by a stealthy fisherman but an irate penguin, furiously attacking the guy rope which it considered was intruding on the territory round its nest. In the morning we had to walk round checking the burrows of our neighbours to retrieve pegs, teaspoons, and any other bits and pieces which they had been able to steal from the camp during the night. Given the chance, they also stole grass nesting-material from each other. We quickly learned to beware of their beaks, with which they could inflict very nasty cuts.

The penguins took the shortest route to the shore, which sometimes led down slopes so steep that they would trip on their webbed feet and bounce down the slope on their breasts, muddying their feathers. When frightened, they went down on all fours, even on the flat, and flapped along in a most uncomfortable manner on flippers and feet.

It is the absence of flight feathers, and the short legs set so far back on the body that it forces them to stand upright, which makes penguins look so absurd. These differences, together with their dense small glossy feathers and the lack of an elbow joint on the wing, cause them to be classed in a different category or superorder from all other birds. But the legs are positioned as they are for faster swimming and each of the other modifications adapts them better for their marine existence. It is believed they lost the power of flight tens of millions of years ago, and like most ancient groups of animals that have survived to the present, they have done so because they have reached a stage of development when they are superbly adapted to their environment.

From the top of the cliffs we could look down through the shallow water and watch them speed along below the surface at up to twenty-five miles an hour. The tremendous power contained in their muscular bodies really showed. They seemed reluctant to venture beyond the kelp beds which ringed the island, and the reason became apparent when we saw the heads of sealions surfacing. Sealions consider a penguin a dainty snack and they are skilled at catching them. When pursued, the penguins porpoise, alternately swimming and leaping through the air. At the time, we speculated whether this might be due to the cloudiness of the water and the need for the penguin to see ahead, but my photographs show that they have their beaks open to breathe.

Thanks to the fishermen the penguin colony is sadly diminished. The old cormorant colonies have completely gone for bait too, with only a few pairs of blue-eyed cormorants nesting on the steepest cliffs. Even the kelp gulls are robbed of their eggs. Simply by walking about the island fishermen affect the breeding success of the penguins, because their burrows are very near the surface. Many collapse naturally with the rain, and the penguin gradually digs deeper, sometimes excavating as much as twenty feet horizontally, to be left with a useable burrow that is only a couple of feet long. An ill-placed foot will go straight through the roof of the burrow and even if the penguin is not trapped inside it will frequently desert. The fishermen must tread on hundreds. Sympathetic as we were to the penguins, it was hard to see where the burrows ran. A moment's inattention and we would step into a burrow. We had travelled half-way round the world to celebrate their way of life on film, and here we were flattening them.

As we returned across the Magellan Straits in a tide that runs at eight knots we were joined by several pairs of beautiful black-and-white Commerson's dolphin. They zig-zagged and tumbled in the bow-wave – quite clearly playing. The Indians used to say that when they whistled as they breathed it meant a storm was coming and that they were warning you to take shelter.

The Indians, of course, fished, and hunted sea-birds and were effective predators. But like all natural predators their numbers depended on the abundance of their prey. Now king crabs are exported all over the world from this area. As the supply dwindles the price goes up and the fishermen try harder to catch those that remain, a route to extinction followed many times in man's short history in South America. Once it was common to see the largest whales in the Fuegian Channels. Now not even their bones are seen.

Compared with the Old World, South America does not possess many large dramatic species of animals. But this was certainly not always the case. In 1833 when Darwin sailed in HMS *Beagle* down the coast of Argentina, while Captain FitzRoy surveyed the harbour of Bahia Blanca, he excavated the fossil bones of nine great quadrupeds from a low cliff at Punta Alta. He formed two important opinions: first, that these giant animals had lived until comparatively recent times, for they were found in association with shells of creatures still found living on the tide-line; second, that in order for so many species to be found that were unknown elsewhere, South America must have been an island. While Captain FitzRoy thought that these monster graveyards were splendid evidence of the extinction brought about by the Flood, Darwin noticed that the land had been elevated and subsequently cut by rivers. He sought another explanation for the death of the giants, and the survival of their diminutive related species. The causes are now much clearer.

Fossil evidence from many different sites shows that Darwin's conjectures were correct. For tens of millions of years South America was an island continent floating across the surface of the earth on its own crustal plate, an ark sustaining its own species which developed to an astonishing diversity out of contact with the rest of the world. In the last fifteen years great advances have been made in understanding how the plates which make up the earth's crust have moved, and the profound changes in the physical appearance and climate of the land which followed.

There are still plenty of unknowns and difficulties. Zoological theory has been rather left behind by the geophysicists. For instance while South American fossils can be dated relative to each other there is so far little absolute dating. It used to be held that South American animals became isolated seventy million years ago when they were cut off from North America. Now it is realised that the separation may have been from Africa when the Atlantic began to open 127 million years ago.

What is in no doubt at all is the dramatic transformation of the continent that has occurred since. It was only after the break with Africa that the main chain of the Andes began to rise. Magma welling upwards from the earth's core thrust aside the ancient sedimentary rocks which folded to form the more recent eastern range of the Andes. This isolated the Amazon basin which previously drained to the west.

No one who has seen the chocolate-brown torrents laden with silt that scour through Chile, or the vast shingle plains of Patagonia, will doubt the effect of erosion. In Cretaceous times alone a depth of seven kilometres of sediment were deposited between the western and eastern ranges to form the Altiplano. (That represents one metre for every 10,000 years.) As the mountains folded and eroded and marched inland the climate varied too. Ice ages came and went, great forests covered Patagonia, and the Amazon basin suffered periods of drought. Whole chains of volcanoes rose and vanished into gravel before the present volcanic chain began to appear about fifteen million years ago. In the highlands of northern Chile and Argentina and in Southern Peru hundreds of thousands of square kilometres were then flooded with volcanic ash to a depth that still reaches 500 metres. Four million years ago the ash eruptions were replaced by lava flows that formed the great volcanoes that smoke in the sky today. One has only to experience an earthquake, to feel the earth heave beneath one's feet, to realise that these cataclysmic processes still continue.

Seventy million years ago, the classical theory goes, there were in South America only three stocks of mammals – the ungulates, the marsupials, and the palaeanodonta (ancient toothless animals). These evolved to a wide variety of orders, families, and genera. Some were extremely large. There was the toxodon which had the form of a guinea-pig but the size of a rhinoceros; the astrapothere that combined the grinding teeth of a herbivore with canines and a trunk; the pyrothere was more like an elephant with trunk and tusks; while the proterotheres repeated some of the evolution followed by horses. The carnivores were all marsupials including a sabre-toothed 'tiger' and a wide variety of 'wolves' and 'cats' similar to their relatives in Australia. Three of the families evolved from the palaeanodonts have surviving members: sloths, anteaters and armadillos. Two are extinct: the ground sloths and the glyptodonts. The ground sloths were the largest animals in South America, some reaching a length of twenty feet, while the glyptodonts were perhaps the most extraordinary. There is the skeleton of one in the Natural History Museum at Buenos Aires. It has a huge domed bony carapace two metres long, immense claws presumably for digging, and a tail spiked like a mace, the most heavily armoured animal that has ever existed. In the same museum is the beak of a phororhacid flesh-eating bird that stood ten feet high and could probably run faster than a horse: the stuff of nightmares.

This strange bestiary was joined about 40 million years ago by rodents and monkeys that suddenly appear in the fossil record. How did they get there when

Sunrise over the island of Cape Horn

The Paine Towers loom above the Patagonian plain

A snowstorm breaks over the Paine Horns

Salto Chico Falls and the Paine range from the south

Osorno volcano with the eroded core of Puntiagudo behind

nothing else did? Possibly by 'waif-dispersal': crossing down a chain of islands by clinging to floating branches. *Where* they came from is less clear. The living South American monkeys differ from those in Africa and Asia by having widely splayed nostrils and prehensile tails, and the oldest fossil primates are found in North America.

The island chain must then have disappeared, until eleven million years ago some raccoon-like animals suddenly show up – again, perhaps, via a chain of islands. Then two to three million years ago the isthmus of Panama rose to form a land bridge to North America. The North American mammals poured south: mastodons, bears, deer, cats, dogs, and finally Man.

Throughout the continent there was a conflict for the survival of the fittest and the placental mammals from the north won. Whether it was because of the larger brain size of the invaders, or their greater adaptability, or the supposed inferiority of the pouch to the placenta, is not clear. The victory was not complete. There was also a migration in the opposite direction, and ground sloths, glyptodonts, armadillos and the Virginia opossum reached North America. Marsupials are still represented in South America by sixty-five species of opossum and the caenolestids, pouchless opossum rats. It is also easy to forget that the overwhelming majority of species comprising insects and plants remained unchanged.

The result is that for its size South America has by far the richest animal population of all the continents: a greater variety of bats and rodents than anywhere else; twice as many bird species as Africa; the survivors from the island stage – the edentates (armadillos, anteaters and sloths); the camelids (guanaco, llama, alpaca and vicuña); over seventy species of monkeys; and the largest number of fresh-water fish.

Other animals have been introduced by Man. First, of course, the dog; then more recently the rabbit, hare, red deer, beaver, etc., and other unintentional immigrants such as the rat and the house-sparrow. But it is likely that he exterminated whole species too.

The last known refuge of one of the South American giants, the mylodon, was discovered in 1893 by Herman Eberhard. He was exploring a large lens-shaped cave on his property near the South Patagonian ice-cap when he found a piece of hairy skin about four feet long. When the skin reached Buenos Aires it appeared so fresh that Florentino Ameghino the doyen of Argentinian palaeontologists rashly published a paper claiming that it was still living.

When I visited the Mylodon Cave, as it is now known world-wide, a fierce cold wind off the ice-cap made it hard to climb the slope to the entrance. In the half light of the cavern with the wind whistling in the trees outside it was not hard to believe that the beast might still live. The cavern is 150 metres wide and 180 deep, formed in a conglomerate rock that looks remarkably like concrete. The floor was a jumble of scientists' and looters' pits. Even the earliest excavations revealed the presence of human bones, mylodon bones and dung, and across the back of the cavern a rock-fall from the roof has formed a barricade of huge boulders which was once fancifully held to be a corral made to confine the animals. The argument as to whether Man killed off the mylodon has been debated ever since Eberhard discovered its bones. The latest radio-carbon dates from the cave show mylodon remains both before and after Man's occupation, the latest being within the last 5643 years.

Analysis of the fossil dung from the cave has also damaged the traditional view of the ground sloth as an animal that reared up on its massive hind-quarters, using its tail as a support, to claw down branches of trees to browse on. In fact it subsisted entirely on a diet of grasses, sedges and similar herbs of moist cool boggy grasslands, a climate unfavourable to Man. What its massive claws and long tongue were used for is now anybody's guess.

One of the many zoological puzzles about South America is why the huge grasslands to the east of the Andes should have so few ungulates – only one deer and no horses. Despite the fact that horses undoubtedly arrived there from North America and were once plentiful, when Pizarro's cavalry fought the Incas in Peru the Indians thought rider and mount were one animal. The reason is almost certainly the presence of the puma, which was once common throughout the continent. It has a special method of killing which is identifiable even on the skeletons of its victims. It jumps on the back of its prey, puts one forepaw on the breast and the other round its neck, then with one swift wrench dislocates the vertebrae, killing the prey stone dead. The size of the prey seems relatively unimportant, and the early settlers of the pampas soon learned that the favourite diet of the puma is horseflesh. Its second preference is for sheep, and in a province of sheep-farmers it is not liked.

Only 150 years ago the puma was found all over the plains of Argentina, and the jaguar, whose chief prey was the capybara, the largest rodent, ranged as far south as the Rio Negro, the northern border of Patagonia. It was recognised that the puma would frequently harass and attack the jaguar, and often kill it, despite the jaguar's superior size and strength. Yet amongst the gauchos the puma was known as a friend, and the extraordinary relationship that pumas have with people is perhaps the strangest of any wild animal.

W.H. Hudson, who grew up amongst the gauchos of the pampas and travelled widely in Argentina, writes, 'It does not attack man, and . . . never hurts, or threatens to hurt, man or child, even when it finds them sleeping. This, however, is not a full statement of the facts; the puma will not even defend itself against man.' This is a statement fully supported by the naturalist Claudio Gay. Hudson quotes a story told to him by an Englishman who came upon a puma when out with a gaucho looking for cattle. 'It sat up with its back against a stone, and did not move even when his companion threw the noose of his lasso over its neck. My informant then dismounted, and, drawing his knife, advanced to kill it: still the puma made no attempt to free itself from the lasso, but it seemed to know, he said, what was coming, for it began to tremble, the tears ran from its eyes, and it whined in the most pitiful manner. He killed it as it sat there unresisting before him, but after accomplishing the deed felt that he had committed a murder. It was the only thing he had ever done in his life, he added, which filled him with remorse when he remembered it. This I thought a rather startling declaration, as I knew that he had killed several individuals of his own species. . . .' If this seems exaggerated it is worth remembering that a man's reputation for prowess in fights and daring was paramount amongst the gauchos. The puma's tears have been recorded by others too.

There is also the story of Maldonada. In 1536 about 2000 inhabitants of Buenos Aires were beseiged in their city by Indians, and according to one account 1800 died of starvation. The corpses, buried just outside the pallisades attracted large numbers of beasts of prey, but despite this people continued to go out into the woods in search of food. Amongst them was the young woman Maldonada. The story is told by Rui Diaz de Guzman a sober-minded historian. She was captured by the Indians and later released, only to be condemned for treachery by the tyrannical Captain Ruiz in charge of the garrison. Maldonada was taken to a wood several miles from the town, tied to a tree, and left there for two nights and a day. A party of soldiers then went to the spot, expecting to find her bones picked clean by the beasts, but were greatly astonished to find Maldonada still alive, without hurt or scratch. She told them that a puma had come to her aid, and had kept at her side, defending her life against all the other beasts that approached her. She was instantly released.

Most South Americans fear the puma; sheep-farmers hate it. The week we arrived in Punta Arenas the Governor of the region announced new measures to be taken to reduce the population of pumas which were claimed to have killed 600 sheep the previous year.

This figure I found extremely suspect. In 1960 I was involved in a survey of animal husbandry in the region and visited a number of farms. The pastures are remote, the weather is severe with heavy snowfalls, shelter is scarce, and the farmer may not see his flock between turning out the ewes in the autumn and lamb-marking in the spring. The puma, or *leon* as it is always called, is a convenient scapegoat for inefficient farming. But despite the persecution it appears to be holding its own in the southern Andes.

Where the puma is constantly shot on sight it has learned to keep out of the way, and I thought it highly unlikely that we would have the opportunity to film one in the wild. Yet it is such an important feature of the ecology of the Andes that I had to obtain film of one somehow. The opportunity came when I met Carlos Venegas, a most good-natured and cheerful ornithologist working for the Patagonian Institute in Punta Arenas.

A few years before, Claudio had been brought a puma cub. The person who had caught it had tried to kill it and had beaten it around the head until it was blind. Claudio had cared for it, its sight had returned, and it was now a magnificent fully-grown animal the size of a young lioness. It was called Patti, for Patagonia. Pumas that are caught as adults never resign themselves to captivity, but those that grow up with people make good pets and in later life do not develop the viciousness that other domesticated big cats usually exhibit.

My plan was to remove Patti from her cage at the Patagonian Institute and take her to a piece of natural beech woodland nearby, with a stream flowing through it, so that we could film her in her natural habitat. The area was fenced only against sheep and Patti would have no trouble getting away if she wanted to. Carlos, who is by nature a supreme optimist, was sure that she would not. Having read Hudson, I was certain at least that we were not likely to get mauled. At the last moment the Institute's security man turned up. He was a classic Latin American: short, squat, moustached, balding, and with a large revolver. I thought he looked considerably more dangerous than Patti.

Carlos led Patti on a strong chain and we followed. My companions did not share my confidence. Hugh had his camera mounted on its tripod over his shoulder with the three sharp points of the legs forward. 'At least I have a chance of stabbing her three times if she goes for me,' he said.

Donaldo MacIver, the third man of my team, an Argentinian who was described by one of my South American friends as the most gaucho gringo he had ever met, unbuckled his enormous sheath-knife.

Patti behaved perfectly. She peered out of cover, sniffed the water, drank, and jumped the stream towards Hugh. The guard fingered his revolver and I hoped that one of us was not going to get shot. But then Patti saw the guanacos.

The guanaco is the largest of the wild camelids to which the domestic llama and alpaca are related. It is also the natural prey of the puma. In the next field there was a family group of captive guanacos dominated by an exceptionally aggressive male who reared on his back legs and ground his teeth at me the moment I got within twenty metres of the fence. Every now and again he would pursue the lesser members of his band, biting their necks until they squealed. I was told that the week before a dog had got into the field and the male had picked it up with its teeth and hurled it to the ground until it was dead. He stood about four feet high at the shoulder and looked down on us with all a camel's disdain. Patti's great thick fawn tail began to twitch.

Donaldo got between the puma and the guanaco, which nearly bit my neck by suddenly leaning over the fence.

Then began a sort of Patagonian bull-fight. Patti would make a dash for the fence, and one of us waving a jacket would get in the way. Carlos got the chain back on her, but it is difficult to stop, or to argue with, a five-foot-long cat. By now her tail was lashing from side to side and I really began to wonder whether we would end up with a demonstration of the puma's method of killing.

The guard was by now waving his revolver and started a running commentary on the lines of, 'You are mad, she will get away and terrorise the district; eat all the children – sheep – dogs . . . Etc.' But Donaldo managed to keep Patti distracted until Claudio got things back under control again by teasing Patti with a heavy rope's-end, much as a kitten is teased with a piece of string. The scale was a bit different: the huge paws swiped at his trouser legs, occasionally ripping them.

We all felt sorry when Patti was put back in her cage again. What an animal! What a thrill to ruffle the fur on a puma's neck!

3

The Paine Towers and the San Rafael Glacier

I think it was the memory of the Paine mountains which drew me back to South America to make *The Flight of the Condor*. I could not forget their vertical spires, the clarity of the light, the raging wind, and the myriads of flowers. Few places that I know possess such a magic. Now I was back.

To my left a 10,600-foot mountain was swathed in a storm of snow. Next to it the Horns of Paine rose to 8760 feet in a curtain of granite cliffs that fell straight to a turquoise lake at sea level furrowed with white by the wind. In front a stark ridge of blade-like vertical peaks rose like the fingers of a hand from a palm of snow – the 'Towers' – and then to my right another black mountain met the cloud. Down beneath its cliffs fell a glacier – white with glimmers of green like an opal – which melted at the snow-line half-way down the slopes. But the peaks were so steep that even some summits were bare rock. Occasionally there was the rumble of an avalanche and a torrent of ice and snow fell in a cascade down a rock face, but more often a whispering roar gave notice of a williwaw streaking white across the lake. That morning the wind was too strong to stand in but in the lulls I could hear the call of the song-sparrow and lark.

Young guanacos with fleecy coats stood on soft rounded hillocks of glacial moraine only 100 yards or so across but still high enough to hide the mountains from the road, which meandered between them like the road to a fairy castle. Beside it were little lakes, some as small and neat as village ponds, every one a different colour and teeming with bird life. Upland geese, white and grey and chestnut with flotillas of downy goslings; smart Chiloé widgeon; red-billed coscoroba swans; buff-necked ibises; coots; the list and variety was endless. Then just when I had come to terms with some small scene, if I raised my eyes the sky was full of the Towers of Paine. The wind raging through their summits brings such a varying burden of cloud that they never look the same twice. Indeed if my eye stayed on the strangely luminous pale granite wall with its splintered cap of black slate I could see the clouds boiling up like steam from a kettle. Each time the contrast of the stark mountains came as a shock.

Amidst the banners of snow streaming from the peaks moved a sharp black speck. A condor. There they were common, but I could not see one without a tingle of excitement that a bird so large could master such a place. When we flopped down on the ground they would float silently down to investigate like giant black moths drawn to the last flicker of a life.

Once there were seventeen whirling in the sky above us as I stood near a ridge, and I was suddenly startled by the *whoof whoof whoof* of huge wings as one flapped over the rock that hid me, blotting out the sky with coffee-coloured feathers. (Only the adults are black.) It was so close that it seemed I could reach up and touch it. There was something very sinister about these great black shapes ten feet across wheeling about one's head waiting for one to die. More like aeroplanes than birds, their necks crane back over their white collars for a better look, the big wedge tails twist and they part the air with the noise of a sailplane. Eagles buck the Patagonian wind with wings swept back like a fighter's, staggering in the gusts; the big condors sail on undisturbed with wingtip primaries streamed back as they head to windward, spreading them like fingers feeling for lift as they turn. I have one of those primaries. It's longer than my forearm and outstretched fingers, as stiff as a batten, and surprisingly heavy. A big condor can weigh twelve kilos, and a friend of mine measured one in Peru that was over three and a half metres in wingspan. If he was right that's longer than the greatest span recorded for the wandering albatross and the Andean condor is the biggest as well as the heaviest bird that flies. More than one sun-bather has woken up with a nasty fright to find a condor flying only a few feet above, and one Scottish girl who was waiting alone in a mountaineering base camp near the Paine was so terrorised by condors over a period of days that she took refuge in a cave. In fact there is no record of them ever attacking a living man, and they always approach prey on foot.

The Paine National Park covers a spread of habitats from the glaciers that descend from the south Patagonian ice-cap, through evergreen and deciduous beech forest, to the Patagonian steppe. They are an elegant example of how geology and climate dictate the forms of life that can be supported.

All mountains have been built by the same geological processes, and the Andes happen to be the best recent example of how they work. The strange Towers of Paine tell part of the story. In the centre of the earth is a molten metallic core. Above that, and roughly equal in depth, is a highly viscous hot mantle of dense dark silicate rock. On top of this, beneath the continents, floats a crust about thirty kilometres thick which is mostly composed of coarse-grained granite. The higher the mountains the thicker the crust to support their weight floating on top of the mantle. Beneath the oceans, on the other hand, the crust is only about eight to ten kilometres thick and is chiefly composed of black, fine-grained basalts. What drove South America away from Africa was the slow eruption of these basalts in a continuous spreading process along the line of what is now the Mid-Atlantic Ridge. The new ocean crust is generated roughly on the mid line of the ocean and spreads out in both directions from it at the rate of about one centimetre per year. But just as South America is floating away from Africa on its continental plate, so it is approaching the Nazca plate beneath the Pacific. This, by a similar process of sea-floor spreading from the East-Pacific Rise, is heading towards South America.

The upwelling at mid-ocean is thought to be caused by convection currents within the mantle lifting heated rock to form the new crust, and at the western edge of South America the reverse takes place: the Pacific plate sinks beneath the Andes. Just to the west of the Andes is the Chile–Peru Trench, a trench deeper than the Andes are high. This is where the descending Nazca plate drags down the edge of the South American continental plate.

As one plate slides beneath the other, several centimetres a year, friction generates enormous quantities of heat, melting some of the rocks in contact. Since this molten material is hotter and thus lighter it moves up through the continental crust. Part of it reaches the surface to form the chain of volcanoes down the Andes – there are over 2000 volcanoes in Chile alone, over fifty of them active. But most of the molten rock never reaches the surface. It cools and comes to rest a few thousands of metres below the surface and crystallises to form enormous masses or intrusions of igneous rock called batholiths. It is the upward thrust of the batholiths which folds sedimentary (layered) rock into ranges like the Andes Cordillera. In time the surrounding rocks are eroded and weathered away and the batholiths are exposed. The granite Towers of Paine are the remains of such a batholith. On top of the pinkish granite is a tilted cap of black slate, the remains of the sedimentary rocks pushed aside when the batholith rose. The vertical cliffs and sweeping curves that look as if the mountains had been carved with an ice-cream scoop are the effects of glaciation.

But the ice in the Paine is retreating, backing down the U-shaped valleys that it has cut, leaving them flooded like fiords, and it is retreating surprisingly fast. The Dickson glacier is backing up at the rate of seventeen metres a year.

As the ice recedes and the naked rock is laid bare the slow process of colonisation by living things takes place. First the lichens grow on the rocks, breaking down the smooth surface by chemical action. The clefts hold soil and moisture for mosses, and in them the seeds of herbs and shrubs can germinate, but the Andean igneous rock is impermeable, and before erosion can carve drainage systems to lower levels, extensive bogs develop, ringed by trees and shrubs dwarfed by the wind. It seems strange that the commonest sphagnum moss is the same species that grows in Scotland, but mosses are amongst the most ancient forms of vegetable life.

If you want to know what the terrain of the super-continent Pangaea looked like about 200 million years ago, look at a south-Andean bog. These bogs can be dangerously deep and the colours are really rather startling with the yellows, greens and rust-reds of the sphagnum species interspersed with clumps of whitish lichen and clusters of pink pernettya berries contrasting with the still blue water of the pools.

Between the mountains and the debris scoured from them by the glaciers are lakes. Their colours are also a surprise, being shades of luminous milky blue.

This is caused by minute particles of silt held in suspension and is characteristic of glacial lakes. Fringing these intensely blue waters is better soil, and there grow woods of dwarf beech whose short twisted trunks lean over beds of delicate ferns and white violets. The trunks of both living and fallen trees are jacketed in moss and the upper boughs support clusters of mistletoe-like mizodendron. They turn an orangey-red which is caught by the gleam of tiny strawberries growing amidst the moss of the fallen trunks. But the most striking plant of all is the ourisia which grows only where it is continually drenched by the spray of waterfalls. The long delicate scarlet bells are covered with jewel-like droplets and nod constantly in the air currents set up by the falling water.

In sheltered valleys grows the finest forest of deciduous high beech. This tree can reach a hundred feet high and twenty feet in girth, but here in the windy Paine the crowns are frequently blown down by gales and in the grass lie the dry and weathered boughs of previous giants. To those used to woods where fallen timber is cleared, for firewood or just through tidy-mindedness, these forests are an extraordinary experience. The fallen trunks make progress very difficult except up and down the slope in the direction the trees fall, but they provide excellent cover for animals. In general, compared with a European forest, the woods are strangely silent, except for the constant rush of wind in the foliage. South American birds sing little, but here you do catch the trill of wrens and the loud scolding chatter of the thorn-tailed rayadito. This courageous little tree-creeper could be called the watch-dog of the forest. It works its way from branch to branch searching for insects, frequently clinging upside down. But if we passed its favourite tree it would flutter down to within two metres of us and scold loudly and continuously, warning everything in the forest that we were about.

Many of the dead standing trees were marked with lines of conical holes as if a giant sewing-machine had run up them. This was the work of the Magellanic woodpecker. Hugh had already spotted a pair of the Chilean flicker by their characteristic undulating woodpecker flight, but the Magellanic woodpecker is much more spectacular. About the size of a jackdaw, the birds are mostly black but the male has a brilliant crimson head and crest.

One day there was a high wind and Donaldo had had a fruitless morning trying to record the calls of guanaco. Hugh had been unable to hold his long lens steady enough to film condors soaring on the ridges and then had sat in his hide on a hilltop for five hours, for at most two shots.

Donaldo and I spent the afternoon looking for the woodpecker in an area where the night before he had glimpsed it fly across the track. It was a most beautiful wooded park-like valley, but like many areas in the Paine it had been burnt over twenty or thirty years ago when it was a sheep farm and the valley was strewn with the grotesque twisted shapes of half-burnt fallen trees. Nothofagus beech burns better than any firewood I have ever come across. One can make an excellent camp fire quickly out of wet green branches, and sadly this has meant the destruction of vast areas of the finest forest. Here the wood was beginning to recover again, but in many places the habitat for birds like the

Magellanic woodpecker has disappeared for ever.

The lines of holes made by the woodpeckers were scattered all around us, but we couldn't see or even hear the birds. We tapped on trees imitating their pecking and listened and searched. Then as I ducked under a curved fallen tree the wood was suddenly full of silent wings. A large brown owl missed me by inches. It perched on a tree twenty metres away blending with the foliage until only its yellow eyes remained, like the grin on the Cheshire cat.

On the way back to our lodging that evening I suggested that we should at least get a shot of the owl. We walked with the equipment up the steep valley thinking that it was a lot of work for one shot even if the owl was still where I had left it, which was unlikely. Then our luck changed. Suddenly we saw two pairs of the Austral parakeet sitting on a stump right in front of us. To see parakeets next to glaciers is as odd as to find penguins in the desert, but equally possible because this parakeet inhabits even Tierra del Fuego. The two pairs were far too absorbed with each other to bother about us. They groomed each other's face and neck, passed each other tasty titbits from the stump, and snuggled up, rubbing shoulders. I was irresistibly reminded of cars parked in a lovers' lane. Then suddenly, to my surprise, the two couples changed partners, and carried on their preening – before evidently deciding they preferred the original pairing, when they swapped back.

A little further up the valley Donaldo recognised the signs where skunks had been digging – one of his girlfriends had once had one for a pet! Almost at once we saw a mother skunk with two babies. With their fluffy tails billowing against the low sun it was hard to tell where one began and the other ended as they snuffled about among the pale yellow anemones and white star orchids that littered the grass. They disappeared under a large rock, but we had already heard the tapping of a woodpecker, so loud that it was as if a woodcutter was at work. Soon we saw the smart black-and-white female undulating through the swaying green foliage. She perched almost immediately over my head as I froze, and then I saw their nest hole. She darted in to feed her young. The female and male called to each other in a loud and unmusical double squawk as they foraged, hammering at the trees with brain-splitting force. Bark flew in all directions, and the male would cock his fiery crimson head and stare into the hole with his brilliant yellow eye before renewing the onslaught further up. The wind whooshed among the tops of the trees which rang with the woodpeckers' harsh cries and the owl still stared just as I had left it two hours before.

Beyond the owl, at the top of the valley, was a spectacular view across Lake Nordenskjold, as blue as turquoise, with the Paine mountains beyond. It had been a marvellous half hour and the frustrations of the day were forgotten; typical of the contrasts of Patagonia. Donaldo returned at dawn the next day in the hope of recording the woodpeckers' calls with less wind and actually saw a puma.

We were in the park for about eight days, and most of that time we concentrated our efforts on filming either the condors or the guanaco.

The guanaco, the wild cousin of the llama and the alpaca, and a relative of the camel, is one of the most successful of the mammalian invaders from North America which crossed the Isthmus of Panama when the two continents were joined. Strangely the guanaco's family has died out in the northern continent, but it survived until recently throughout the Andes and the west coast of South America from sea level to a height of 13,000 feet. Few animals other than its enemy the puma exceed this range. The guanaco's other enemy is Man, and with the advent of the rifle its numbers were cut down so severely that it no longer exists in many of its former habitats. Only in the last ten years has there been any improvement in its numbers in protected areas, especially in Tierra del Fuego and the Paine park.

The guanaco was fundamental to the life of the Ona and Tehuelche Indians, furnishing them meat, skins and bone for implements. Antonio Pigafetta in 1520 was one of the first Europeans to see a guanaco when shown one by the Indians which he called Patagones: big-feet – from their guanaco moccasins – and thus Patagonia.

As the males stood in heraldic postures on hilltops, outlined against the blue cliffs of the mountains behind, we were struck more by their grace than their oddity. Their soft dark ears outlined in white standing up above their large brown eyes always looked to me like exclamation marks and made them appear permanently surprised. Each dominant male kept his family group of females and yearlings to a well-defined territory and stood guard over it, watching from higher ground. The guanaco's hearing is wonderfully acute, and I well remember in the forests of Tierra del Fuego how our first knowledge that they were there was usually when we heard the high-pitched bray like a peal of laughter. Then it was too late, as they would slip silently and invisibly away.

Twenty years ago there was not a guanaco to be seen near the Paine mountains. Now they were everywhere, and we could easily approach within about 100 yards even on foot. Our problems now were not with the animals but with the wind, whose chilling, desiccating effect is the cause of the hummocky vegetation of cushion plants. This form of growth helps to conserve heat and moisture, but we found it difficult and tiring to walk over. The guanacos had no such problem, bounding up the steep slopes with agility and grace on their soft-padded feet.

As it was spring most of the birds in the park either had chicks or were nesting. One of the most amusing sights was to see a couple of dozen tiny ostrich chicks scurrying after their long-legged parent. These were the Darwin's (or lesser) rhea. It is worth pointing out that there are three totally different kinds of flightless birds in South America: the rheas, the penguins, and the steamer-ducks. The rheas are related to the ostriches of Africa and the emu, cassowary, and kiwi of Australasia. It was once a puzzle how these birds of a common ancestry had been able to cross from one continent to another, since they could not fly, but of course it was the giant continent that split up and divided their ancestors.

The periscope-like necks of the guanaco and rhea adapt them to life in open country. The rhea can stay 'hull-down' on the horizon with only its head appearing between the bushes, and if an enemy approaches it freezes and its blueish-grey mottled nondescript plumage makes it almost indistinguishable from all the other rounded humps that form the vegetation. The Indians and then the gauchos hunted this and the more northern, larger, species with the bolas – three round stones joined to a central point by rawhide cords. One stone was held in the hand and the other two whirled round the head and released to entangle the head and then feet of the running bird. I once watched such a hunt. The rhea is very fast and has an amazing ability to double back on its tracks just when it seems about to be caught. It raises its wings alternately as if to try to get extra speed from the wind, and can suddenly disappear by dropping into the undergrowth. The chicks were surprisingly fast and had no hesitation in dashing into and across water. The only way that Hugh managed to film them was by catching the slowest chick of a brood and then trapping it within a rampart of bushes so that its high-pitched peeping called the adult to return to it. Of course he released it back to the brood when he had finished filming.

Rheas have a curious social structure. The males tend the nest, in which as many as five or six females lay fifty or even more eggs. The male incubates the eggs and later takes care of the young, but the females may lay in more than one nest. A rhea's egg is big, about 125 millimetres across, with a tough thick shell. Remembering the strange creatures that peopled South America until the land-bridge formed to the north it is interesting to speculate what the rheas' enemies were while it was evolving. Perhaps the giant flightless predatory birds?

One of the most beautiful aspects of the Paine was the immense number of waterfowl congregating and nesting on the lakes and marshes. It was impossible not to be moved, however reluctantly, by the sight of huge flights of upland geese against the black mountainside, sun streaming through their white secondaries and making the yellow feet of the darker females glow against the sunburst behind. South American geese, although resembling true geese, are in fact more closely related to some of the ducks such as the shelduck. They are usually to be seen grazing, and eight geese eat as much as a sheep. Throughout the temperate grasslands of the south they are so abundant that they are considered a plague by the farmers who in the past have made the mistake of shooting their enemies the foxes. One reason that there are so many is that their flesh is so tough as to be almost inedible.

Seen through binoculars at close range the plumage of these birds is very striking, particularly the ashy-headed geese, which we saw swimming with their broods on little ponds in the woods. They had grey heads, chestnut backs, and black-and-white barred sides. Out on the bigger lagoons in the open were flamingoes, and black-necked swans breasted the small breaking waves with their cygnets riding safely on their backs between their wings. There were many kinds of duck too: pintail, teal, shovellers, and the Chiloé widgeon, a dabbling duck with a lovely three-syllable whistle. This noise, with the plaintive metallic honk of the buff-necked ibises and the gabbling of the geese are for me the most characteristic sounds of Patagonia.

Beside one of the lagoons I found the nest of an upland goose near a bush, a little pool of down and breast feathers clinging together despite shivering like a jelly in the tearing gusts of wind. Parting the down gently I discovered five eggs the colour of a hen's but twice the size. They were as warm as if the female had only just left them, yet I had not seen her, and it was so cold that I was wearing ear-flaps and gloves.

The condors were ridge-soaring again. An immature black-chested buzzard eagle, a bird that anywhere else would be considered huge, within metres of me, level with my face, soaring in the gusts. I could see the outline of every feather on its head and neck and the sky reflected in its bright eye. For a moment I was afraid of its talons, but it was hunting hares. Above, two condors collided in a tumble of wings and another flip-rolled to ward off an aerial challenger with its feet. They watched each other closely as each searched the ground below for carrion, their shadows sweeping across the hillsides and mountains.

A female guanaco stood on a ridge tail-on to the wind that sent shock-waves through her shaggy coat. She bent and sniffed at something on the ground. The guanacos had been dropping their foals at night but the previous night had been exceptionally cold and Hugh guessed that something was wrong. He found two dead foals and a third that was dying, unable to rise to its feet. Next day this foal too was dead. Hugh watched and waited all day in his hide and filmed the mother driving away a condor intent on her dead foal – it hopped nervously sideways and spread its wings which were wider than the guanaco, an impressive demonstration of the bird's size. The next day the mother was sitting in the same spot but she started nervously to her feet as we walked up through the cushion plants. Lying among the flowers was a bundle of disjointed dry bones wrapped in a soft furred hide turned inside-out. The eye sockets were empty in the furry muzzle. When we look at an animal it is the eye that responds and nothing is so dead as an eyeless head, yet the mother had a parental bond stronger than even the eyeless sockets could sever. A day later she was still there, though the condors ignored her and fed on such scraps of flesh as remained. She must have been weakening from hunger yet she would not abandon her vigil. Meanwhile, on some bleak cliff the condors too had young and they also had to feed.

The last thing that Hugh filmed in the Paine park was a mother guanaco and her foal with their golden fleeces shining against the glaciers and granite. The foal was newly born and nuzzled up and down the mother's flank instinctively searching for a teat. It tried her rump, then between her forelegs. It looked very frail, wobbling on its legs in the tearing wind of the ridge. The mother moved nervously and the calf tried again. At last mouth and teat connected and I found myself relaxing. The foal would live.

The Chilean national coat of arms is a shield supported on the right by a condor and on the left by a huemul, in real life two peculiarly inelegant beasts. The huemul looks like a mule with cloven hoofs, reflecting the controversy surrounding its status that is enshrined in its scientific name: *Hippocamelus* (horse-camel). Its name changed twenty-one times between 1782 and 1902 and few people even now can spell it! It is known in English as the Andean deer, the huemul being the southern species which lives in the uppermost forest of the mountains of southern Chile. Once it was common, but like the puma, it is by nature an extraordinarily confiding animal, and its habit of simply staring at anyone who approaches, while munching a mouthful of forage, has made it extremely easy to shoot. There are few Chileans who have seen it in the wild other than down the sights of a rifle. The deer do not survive in captivity and they are now officially an endangered species with an estimated population of 500 to 1500 individuals. The ratio of one to three in this estimate illustrates the difficulty of guaging the population of an animal which survives only where Man seldom goes.

Near the town of Coihaique, 400 miles north of the Paine mountains, there is now a tiny reserve where about thirty-five animals remain at the top of a very steep scarp above the Rio Claro. To get there we drove up a poor track through the burnt remnants of what had been a forest. Nowhere is the destruction of the southern beech forest more sadly visible than here. In the 1930s huge areas of fine forest were burnt to make poor pasture. Often the fires were allowed to burn right up the mountain sides far above the area useful, however marginally, for ranching, and one fire was said to have burned for three months. Despite official prohibition, they are still burning forest in Chile. At Rio Claro it was a depressing sight to see nothing but bleached fallen trees and to talk to smallholders who said that they could not make a living on the poor land that resulted. The erosion caused by destroying the forest has been so great that the port of Aisen has silted up and a new port had to be built.

The guard had said that the huemuls worked their way down the slopes during the day towards the river at the bottom. But at first light Hugh spotted one a third of the way down the mountainside. He set off up the extremely steep scree slope carrying his heavy camera and tripod, stalking it from cover to cover. The huemuls here have been shot at steadily for the last fifty years and have learned to distrust Man. I didn't think Hugh had much chance, but we kept him informed of the animal's movements by walkie-talkie. From the vantage-point of the hut set on a knoll we had a much better view of the mountain than he. He had climbed about 1000 feet when a large stone slid from beneath his feet and startled the animal which began to make off, using its heavy hind-quarters and short legs to thrust itself effortlessly higher. Hugh managed to get some good steady shots despite his lack of breath and thumping heart. So far as we knew, it was the first time that the animal had ever been filmed, and with a bit of luck if the films are shown on Chilean television it will encourage them to look after it and its lonely world of forest and mountain peaks.

Ice is the major force that erodes mountain ranges, and one of the most accessible large glaciers in Chile is also the glacier nearest the equator to reach the sea: the San Rafael glacier, in latitude 42° 42′ South. In the same latitude north, Chateau Mouton Rothschild is grown. Normally it takes a round trip of a week by boat to reach the glacier for a few hours, but in the thirties the Chilean railway company had the mad idea of building a luxury hotel there. Its ruins remain and so does a derelict airstrip. I had been tipped off about this, so we flew in from Coyhaique, dodging between the mountains and the clouds, taking our inflatable boat.

The San Rafael Glacier is a mere remnant compared to what it must once have been, but it is still impressive. It is four kilometres wide at its front where the ice cliff is forty to sixty metres high. It stretches back about twenty-five kilometres into the mountains, a white river poured down the bottom of the dark forested valley.

At sea-level it never snows and here the surface of the glacier was uncovered: a fantastic tumult of pinnacles and crevasses, spires and hollows, caused by the compression and thawing of the ice. The glacier ended in a large tidal lagoon ten kilometres across and almost landlocked, containing very large numbers of icebergs floating in pack-ice. Were it not for the dark mountains beyond it would have seemed like Antarctica.

From our little rubber boat the ice was extremely impressive. It had sheer smooth vertical cliffs the deep blue of the ocean or a high-altitude sky, flecked with streaks of white like cirrus. Huge blocks collapsed suddenly into the water with no warning, causing miniature tidal waves, and geysers of spray flung high into the air. The water below the ice was turbulent with eddies where the melt-water gushed up from beneath and to add to our feeling of insecurity every now and then the sea would boil and rumble and bergs would surface from underneath the ice cliff, their jagged spires shooting high into the air, twisting and falling again in rings of white foam. These under-water bergs were as clear as glass and as greeny-blue. We made several passes close under the cliff of the glacier to film it and then cautiously made our way through the tinkling brash-ice – which threatened to puncture our boat with its sharp points – towards an island at the north end of the glacier. This was an excellent vantage point from which to film the collapsing ice cliff.

A glacier like this flows some hundreds of metres in a year and grinds away the rock at about two millimetres a year – two metres in 1000 years. But 1000 years is the twinkling of an eye in geological time. Where the ice had ground over our island it had cut grooves in the rock and had sheared it away on the downstream side. On top of the island were scattered boulders, stones and pebbles, debris from the rock walls of the valley, just as they had been deposited by the retreating ice. Some were placed as carefully on the ledges of the sloping rock as if by hand. Many of them were round, which showed that they must have been eroded in the meltwater stream beneath the ice, a wonderful mixture of kinds of rock: granite, slate, marble, basalt – all colours and sizes, each from a different part of the range.

We were awed by the sound of the glacier: sharp cracks almost like shots and a huge booming thunder that can be heard ten miles away. It was very hard to tell which section was going to collapse next, or when, despite the crazy outward angle of some of the leaning pinnacles. But we needed good shots of falling ice.

We were returning in our boat to film the bluest section in a better light when I noticed that one particularly large slab looked as if it was going to give way. The faintest trickle of white chips cascaded at the edges. We continued to approach it.

We were about 100 metres off when the ice began to fall. We had half a second's notice as small pieces collapsed near the bottom and Hugh got the camera running. Then a cube the size of a four-storey house thundered into the water, the glass-blue sliding into a white ring of spray from which a shower of ice was fired out sideways like an explosion. I kept on driving slowly towards it until I saw a five-foot-high breaking wave heading for us. I held course for what I thought was another second to let Hugh finish the shot, shouted to him to hang on and was glad of the power of the twenty-five horse-power motor as we sped out of reach of the wave. Both of us were very excited to have got such a good shot, and could not stop laughing with relief at our narrow escape.

One of the problems with filming is that so many things can go wrong between taking the shot and seeing the print of the negative. Even a minor piece of grit in the camera gate can ruin a shot and most producers and cameramen have been through the galling experience of disaster, ranging from forgetting to put film in the camera to having the film break in the laboratory processing bath or even being stolen on its way to the processing laboratory. A most important duty of the home base is to send a rushes report by cable as soon as the print can be viewed. We were often so far from international airports, or civilisation of any kind, that frequently we would have to wait weeks until we could send off a parcel of film. It is uneasy for one's nerves to know that there is no chance of going back for a retake.

Of all the film that we shot at San Rafael the only shot to be spoilt was this one of the falling berg, of all things by static electricity which painted a waving blue veil over both sides of the shot! It was almost as if the electricity of our excitement had penetrated the camera to undo our efforts. On the film I could see how quickly I had turned the boat away from the falling ice – much too quickly. One's mind seems to run at ten times normal speed in such circumstances.

The next day was windless and sunny. Our luck with the weather still held, for this area too is renowned for its wet banks of cloud, though the climate is far milder than the Paine, as it is over 300 miles further north. We took the rubber boat to the forest north of the lagoon, weaving between the bergs. The sea was completely flat and the giant blue bergs looked quite preposterous sitting on perfectly symmetrical reflections. The small ones were melted into extraordinary shapes full of holes and blade-like edges and they glittered in the sun. The shore was strewn with fallen trees and a dense growth came right up to the high tide mark. We drew up the boat feeling like castaways on a shore brought by magic from the tropics. This was the southern extremity of the

Valdivian rain forest. The confusion of vegetation was almost impenetrable, a luxuriant tangle of beech and climbing bamboo covered with mosses and ferns. The giant prickly leaves of *gunnera* opened like outsize rhubarb towards the light of the shore and the trees were hung with red flowers: fuchsia, coicopihue, wild currant, and the shy blooms of others I did not know half hidden in the moss. Everything dripped with moisture and was the more extraordinary for being within sight of large icebergs that had run aground on the shore. A pair of ringed kingfishers, large birds with blue-grey crests and chestnut bellies with a smart white collar, rattled musically at each other from their perches close above our heads.

I used a fallen tree as a bridge from the shore into the forest where the trunk became covered in mosses, some ten centimetres long. It disappeared into an amorphous carpet of moss that collapsed disconcertingly beneath me, the lichens were so thick that it reminded me of an underwater scene. I could hear an occasional rumble from the glacier but the forest was full of the calls of the fio-fio (white-crested elaenia) searching for insects amongst the branches, uttering its onomatopoeic call: feeo-feeo. Then a bird like a scaled-up robin with a black cap and a tail cocked straight upwards hopped between the bamboo stems only a couple of metres away eyeing me curiously. It called with a ringing musical chuckle but the noise seemed to come from behind me – an accomplished ventriloquist. It disappeared as suddenly as it called and the sound was to haunt us in the wet woods wherever we went. It was a chucao, one of the six species of the family *Rhinocryptidae* that are exclusively found in Chile and are the most characteristic voices of the Chilean countryside. They are quite extraordinarily difficult to film as they always skulk in the undergrowth.

We woke next morning to find a steady drizzle and the cloud sunk low on the mountains. Hugh used the drier spells to film the green-backed firecrown humming-bird feeding on the honey-suckle-like blooms of the fire bush. This extraordinary little bird even reaches Tierra del Fuego and has developed the capacity to hibernate, passing the coldest months in a torpor, hanging inside thick bushes. Here it completed the illusion that we had found a glacier in the tropical jungle.

Sharp at six o'clock we heard the sound of an engine and our little plane came hedge-hopping in over the forest. The weather was so thick that we had never expected it to arrive. Soon we were heading north once more, leaving behind the black channels and forests which exert such a strange magnetism on anyone who has the tenacity and the luck to travel amongst them.

2

PREVIOUS PAGE Weatherbeaten islands
near Cape Horn

LEFT Lichen and
sphagnum moss
BELOW Prickly heath
(Pernettya)

3

OPPOSITE
Navarin Island;
sphagnum bog
and evergreen
southern beech forest

OPPOSITE Evergreen
southern beech forest

RIGHT Male kelp goose
and juvenile
BELOW Magellanic
penguins

7

8

LEFT Ourisia, the 'waterfall flower'
BELOW Low beech forest contorted by the wind

9

ABOVE The South
Patagonian Ice-cap

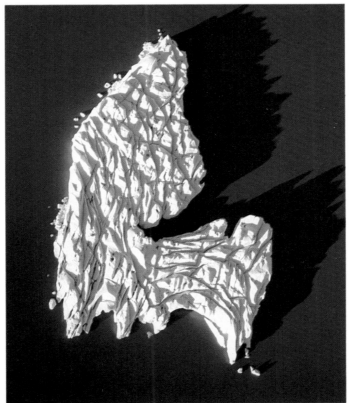

Iceberg in a fiord

PREVIOUS PAGE
The Paine Horns
with Lake Pehoé

LEFT   Guanacos

OPPOSITE
The Paine Towers

17

OPPOSITE ABOVE
Black-necked swans
OPPOSITE BELOW
Condors

RIGHT Puma and
Paine mountains

OVERLEAF   Upland geese

Magellanic pea

Native anemone

20

4

The Temperate Rain Forest and the Volcanoes of South Chile

Eight hundred miles north of Cape Horn, the sunken mountain range which forms the scattered fringe of islands bordering the Pacific coast of South America is united to the mainland. Much older than the main chain of the Andes, it runs north up the coast of Chile. But before it can do this it is cut, at Puerto Montt, by a narrow channel which divides off the large island of Chiloé, about half the size of Wales.

Chiloé was our next destination. It has a reputation for witchcraft, wooden buildings, poverty, seafood and rain. In the summer it attracts large numbers of student hitch-hikers from the capital, Santiago, drawn by the beautiful fishing villages and the scenery of the sheltered eastern coast, but we were heading for the west, which is still partly unexplored.

The national parks of Chile are run by CONAF, the national forestry corporation, which falls within the responsibility of the Ministry of Agriculture. Few governments realise, or are prepared to concede, what a bad deal the natural history of their country receives if its guardianship is put in the hands of those whose job is to cut down trees and dig up the land. In Latin America, where short-term profit is valued over planning, the future for wildlife is bleak. It suffers for the same reasons that ours did in the last century, and indeed still did only a generation ago.

Chile is at present governed with economic policies of the rigorous monetarist 'Chicago School' of Milton Friedman. Its doctrines are being applied with great vigour: the division of wildlife had just had its entire research budget cut, and the Ministry was seriously considering selling off many of the national parks. (We must not forget that the equivalent is also happening in North America under the Reagan administration and is threatened in Snowdonia.) When I asked a CONAF employee why, he replied sadly that the government considered that any government enterprise was a drain on the government exchequer, and that any private enterprise either produced taxes or at worst nothing. Fortunately there are many in Chile who also take the view that the government – regardless of its political complexion – is also the guardian of the nation's heritage, of which the landscape and wildlife of the country are an

49

important part. They were greatly encouraged that the BBC should have sent me to record their wildlife, as this demonstrated its value in a very practical way. Sadly the attitude of the local public, up until recently, has been exclusively predatory. Wildlife is to eat, to throw stones at, or shoot.

The cuts had affected both the project to conserve the huemul (which as I mentioned appears on the national coat of arms) and a study of the sea otter, which we now hoped to film. It is a sad fact that very few graduates in zoology from Latin American universities are prepared to go out in the field and get their boots dirty looking for animals. They prefer classification work in museums or desk jobs which mean they can stay close to their wives and families in the comfort of the city. There is no tradition of fieldworkers, either amateur or professional, and it was depressing to discover that Carlos Cabello, who had been working with the marine otter in the field for four years, had been transferred to administrative duties on the mainland as a result of the cuts. However, at least he had not lost his job, and I persuaded his boss to let him take us to his study area.

The Pacific marine otter of Chile is officially described as endangered, but it is still illegally hunted for its skin. It has a wide range, from Cape Horn to Peru, and there is such a scarcity of mammalian life in the channels of Patagonia that I was anxious to get some good footage of what is locally called the chungungo, a much smaller animal than its Californian cousin.

Carlos Cabello greeted us with enthusiasm. He was dark and bearded, with wistful eyes behind steel-rimmed glasses and a rather hesitant manner. He directed us to a village, or rather a scattered handful of farms, on the northern Pacific coast of Chiloé. It was called Pumillahue – literally, the place of the small puma – which was odd because pumas do not occur on the island. The intention was that we should pick up a boat there to reach his research site further south.

It could be done in two ways. If it was calm we would go by boat, but if rough we had to go with horses from a different town. It seemed to me quite straightforward, we would go by boat if we could, but only take as much equipment as could be brought out by horse. This meant leaving our own boat and motor behind. This required about two hours of explanation.

Carlos could not understand why we had to be in such a hurry. I tried to explain that I had five weeks of filming scheduled to the day, but it was beyond his comprehension. The scale of what we were doing and the professional standard which we had to maintain were impossible to communicate.

It took us over four hours actually to get to the boat, a solid-looking thirty-foot fishing launch with a forty-five horse-power motor, but almost as soon as we got going from the tiny cove things improved. Even as we left we passed a stack rock with a group of southern sealions. Most of them crashed into the water, but one huge male remained to glare his defiance at us over a female and two cubs. We motored past impressive cliffs and outlying rocks and watched the Pacific grin white through its milky green. A never-ending stream of sooty shearwaters flew past us heading north.

Two hours later and fifteen kilometres to the south we handed the cameras and rucksacks ashore. The boat surged against a very jagged rock beside a beach just wide enough to pull it up with a wooden capstan. A narrow path led up through a dense growth of forest covered with mosses and epiphytes, thick with climbing bamboo. A gently sloping beach extended for a mile to the north littered with sea wrack and shattered tree-trunks. There was no sign of any human occupation in the whole landscape.

We were all enchanted by the appearance and wildness of the place and had an energetic time carrying all the supplies up a steep slope to a fine shingle hut on the top of the bluff.

By early afternoon we had lunched and as it was a fine calm day Carlos led myself and Hugh to look for the chungungo. Hugh was carrying his camera on its tripod set up for instant action. Carlos looked doubtfully at the camera and asked whether Hugh wanted to carry it like that as we were going through the bush. Hugh, who very much dislikes anyone interfering with his equipment, said that was what he usually did.

Twenty yards from the house we plunged into a soaking-wet bamboo thicket and then forest. Carlos promptly got lost.

We struggled on through the forest, climbing fallen logs, pushing through thickets, crawling under vines. The bamboo hanging down like lianas kept hooking over the camera. Hugh stopped to film a chucao while Carlos looked for the track. The bird either hid, displaying its powers as a ventriloquist that made it almost impossible to locate, or it hopped so close that Hugh could not focus on it. This morning its call sounded distinctly like a laugh.

From crawling we were suddenly rock-climbing down a precipice. We crossed a stream where it entered the tail of a cliff-shrouded bay and climbed over large jagged boulders for 100 yards. I was beginning to think it made a pretty good obstacle course when we arrived at a choice of climbing either a twenty-five foot vertical rock-face or an almost vertical bank of vegetation.

Hugh's main preoccupation was not to damage his camera. We had already split the camera and tripod – a most unusual thing for Hugh to do. Now we dismantled the camera itself and shared it between our two small rucksacks. We had to crawl on our stomachs in the wet moss beneath thick bamboo to get up the cliff.

We emerged on a rock facing the ocean again. Hugh found a suitably low rock platform where he was not silhouetted against the sky. He was just extending the legs of the tripod when an otter surfaced thirty yards from where we stood. We scrambled to put the camera together. The otter lay on its back with its paws in the air eating a crab. With my binoculars I could see its whiskers. In fifteen minutes we had seen otters four times and Hugh had got several shots including one of an otter climbing up on a rock and being washed off it again repeatedly by waves. Carlos had certainly brought us to the right place even though it had been hard to reach.

Lutra felina, the Chilean marine otter, is rather smaller than the European otter and exclusively maritime. The main difference in these animals' behaviour appeared to be that they spend comparatively little time out of the water on rocks, probably because of the fierceness of the seas on this open coast. Their small size made them hard to see in any broken water, and it surprised me how Hugh could pick out their dark pointed heads at a distance. They went from feeding straight to their holts, caves beneath the piles of large rocks; surfacing beneath the kelp which calms the surf, and scrambling quickly up in predictable places. They fed mostly on orangey-red crabs, bringing the big ones ashore but eating the small ones while floating on their backs. Their spraints (faeces) are full of pieces of shell – some as big as a finger-nail, which must be painful to excrete!

Carlos had been working on the population of otters along this stretch of coast, spending twenty minutes at each designated observation post to note the numbers of otters he saw. What surprised us was how little he appeared to know about their behaviour or the position of their holts, which may be either nests or just places to rest. I began to suspect that the practicalities – organising the boat, building the hut, keeping the trails clear, etc. – had taken up most of his study time.

Near the hut green-backed firecrown humming-birds chased each other at high speed around the native berberis and fuchsia. They spent so much time fighting that I wondered how they could make up the energy they expended, but their food – nectar – has a high sugar content. The male had a white dot behind the eye, but as humming-birds go they were a bit drab. The wonder is that they were there at all where it was still so cold. It is noticeable how many of the southern shrubs have reddish flowers to attract pollinating humming-birds – possibly because there are so few bees. Birds can see colours, and are attracted by reds, while insects are attracted by the ultra-violet part of the spectrum, so where birds do not pollinate you do not find many bright red flowers. Another extraordinary little bird caught my attention as it skulked between the bamboo thickets. It was even smaller and slimmer than a wren with a reddish cap and a pair of enormously long tail feathers, twice the length of its body, which undulated behind it as it flew like the pennant on some mediaeval masthead. Des Mur's wire-tail is the smallest bird of these forests, and looks as improbable as its name.

Besides the penetrating sounds of the fio-fio and the cackle of the chucao this forest had a new call which at first sounded remarkably like the irritated yapping of a small terrier puppy. This was the huet huet, a bird bigger than a large thrush and, if it is possible, even more infuriating to try to film than the chucao. It rarely flies, but creeps round the floor of the darkest parts of the forest, and it is both extremely shy and very curious. Look for it, and you will never find it, but sit still where you have heard it calling and frequently it will suddenly appear only a couple of metres away, an almost black bird with a red cap and breast and outsized feet for scratching like a chicken in the leaves. Like the chucao its tail is carried so erect that it even inclines towards the head, and locally all these birds are called tapaculos which Darwin translated as 'cover your posterior' birds.

Hugh came back at seven that evening, having spent twelve hours sitting behind his camera concentrating every second in case he missed an otter. He reported that he had got two or three good shots including a close-up of one eating – which I had written into the script but had been doubtful that we would manage to get. He was also excited to have seen a young male and female which had been romping and rolling on a patch of yellowish seaweed on a rock. To get closer shots he had to be the other side of the rocky inlet, and that meant cutting a trail up and over an islet which was separated from the mainland by a strip of sand.

Donaldo and I set off to cut the way next morning, hampered by the lack of a machete. The only way up the cliffs of the islet was in an angle completely filled with a tangle of bamboo. We hacked a tunnel and scrambled over and then under the growth. It reminded me of the ascent to Conan Doyle's lost world. I had dreamed as a schoolboy of hacking my way up a cliff to a plateau where nobody had been before.

We came to a twenty-foot rock-face which fortunately had just enough hand-holds and a couple of long bamboo lianas in the right place. We were soon at the top, but the top was almost impenetrable. It was a mixture of dwarf beech, some relative of the pineapple, flowering shrubs, *gunnera* with ten-foot diameter spiky leaves, and, of course, the climbing bamboo. It was raining hard and the constant hacking and scrambling was strenuous, but I found myself enjoying it. Soon, much to Hugh's surprise, we called him by radio from the top of the cliff.

It took us a little time to find a way down the cliff to the site for the hide. It was either sheer rock or a very thick tangle of dwarf beech. We then cleared the track properly on our way back. It rained hard all day and half the next and the otters were too wary of the hide. Our efforts had been in vain.

One evening after a hot afternoon I walked along the desolate beach to the river to have a swim. Where it crossed the beach it was about twenty yards wide and I followed it up into the completely tropical-looking forest. The only way to progress was to walk in the water and I had to swim across two or three times. Once I saw a snipe feeding by the water's edge, but nothing else and it was so cold in the water that I was a little afraid that I might get into difficulties. So I returned, teeth chattering, to my clothes. On the way back across the beach I saw a pudu, the dwarf forest deer of the Andes. It was grazing at the top of the sand; a female, the size of a largish dog, dark brown with golden-brown ears.

Chile is much like an island from the point of view of its wildlife. To the north lies the Atacama Desert, to the west the Pacific, to the east the Andes, and to the south the ice and fiords of Patagonia. It has thus been host to a large number of its own endemic species such as the chucao and huet huet. Although the pudu is also found nearby in Argentina, Peru and Bolivia it is primarily a Chilean species. Once they used to run in small herds but their numbers have fallen greatly in recent years. I walked in an arc towards the pudu's dark brown beady eyes. She lifted her head, I stopped, and she continued to graze. I got within ten yards and then her mate in the bush caught my scent and gave a high-pitched warning like the cry of a bird. The pudu at once started sniffing the air. She must have been incredibly short-sighted or else completely indifferent to my presence, as I was standing against the open sea and sky. She ambled off to leave the beach a far less lonely world.

Although pudus are frequently kept as pets in Chile (despite their official status as a protected species) almost nothing is known about their life in the wild. But their habitat of the dense bamboo forests which once covered the whole of the south of Chile has been dramatically reduced. The Chilean government even then was putting out tenders for most of the forest of Chiloé to be cut for chip-board.

We had had endless discussions about how and when to leave. As even a moderate breeze was considered too rough for the boat, horses were sent for and arrived, much to our surprise. They were tiny ponies, but we were later to admire their stamina and the determination with which they would plough through belly-deep mud and swift rivers.

The following morning it was pouring with rain again – Chiloé was doing its best to live up to its reputation. We hauled the boat higher up and loaded the horses. There were only the most rudimentary pack-saddles nailed together with enormous nails. We packed our precious equipment inside plastic bags in suitcases and they were sewn up into fishing-net and hung on the horses. We set off north along the beach like a party of Cornish wreckers.

It was blowing quite hard from the west and the breakers were a fine sight as they rolled in throwing a debris of kelp and crab-shells high up the beach. There were flocks of Magellanic oystercatchers running to and fro after the waves, on legs that looked much too short, seizing razor-shell clams from the sand. The debris of their work lay in piles of millions of empty shells cast higher up by the waves. There were also enormous barnacle shells six inches long and timbers hollowed out by the teredo worm until they were just empty husks. The storm and the mist closed in around us as we tramped on.

We made a steep muddy detour through forest filled with ferns and moss and flowers and out through bamboo to the coast again. As we descended a steep path to the beach a load slipped back. The cord acted as a girth constricting the horse's lower belly and it was off. It pranced and bucked and the load swung round beneath it, entangling it still further. Showers of sand flew backwards and hooves crashed against two precious suitcases. There was a Nagra tape-recorder in one case worth over £1200, and two walkie-talkies worth £1500 in the other. Suddenly a large fish flew through the air, then another and another. The fish that we had caught and smoked were in a sack beneath those hooves. All of us were helpless with laughter at the sight of the flying fish and it was some time before I could do anything to save our gear. Luckily the horse came my way and I grabbed it, being rather uncertain what to say to a bucking horse in Spanish. We recovered the battered suitcases, not daring to undo them in the sand and rain.

About three in the afternoon we reached the river Chepu feeling very wet and rather footsore. There were two boats waiting for us. We haggled a price, unloaded the horses, and swam them across the river. The driver of our boat took a hearty pull at his outboard starting-rope and it came straight off in his hand, so we took it in turns to row five miles against the current. Our slow progress gave me a good opportunity to examine the forest which had been drowned by the sinking of the river valley in the 1960 earthquake.

I remember in 1961 watching the red glow of the crater of volcano Calbuco near Puerto Montt lighting up the clouds by night and the coils of yellowish smoke towering above it by day. I had persuaded the airforce to take me up in a helicopter to film the eruption from the air. We clattered up over the lake and round the volcano. A stream of lava had cut through the forest, which was still smoking, shattered houses and bridges lay on either side of the flow and we flew in and out of the stifling sulphurous smoke hanging over the still-molten lava like a dragon-fly over a red-brown pond. In retrospect I had always thought it was one of the craziest things I had done.

It was six months after the major earthquake of 1960: probably the biggest quake to rock the earth this century – a two hundred mile long stretch of the Chilean coastline sank two metres into the Pacific, the globe rang like a gong for a fortnight with the vibrations, and tsunami waves crossed the Pacific to drown numbers of people in Japan. At Niebla, a town at the mouth of a river which had suddenly become deep enough to make the city of Valdivia a port, the giant waves had left nothing but the kerbstones standing, and fishing-boats had been hurled hundreds of yards to be embedded in the wreckage of a steel mill. I was not surprised, when we felt a minor tremor, that everybody ran for the door.

In 1853 Charles Darwin experienced a great earthquake at Valdivia which destroyed the nearby town of Concepción . . .

'A bad earthquake at once destroys our oldest associations; the earth, the very emblem of solidity, has moved beneath our feet like a thin crust over a fluid; – one second of time has created in the mind a strange idea of insecurity, which hours of reflection would not have produced.' When he later discovered sea-shells fourteen thousand feet up in the Andes he was deeply impressed by the scale of the forces involved. Such are the effects of the Nazca plate sliding down beneath the continental crust.

Calbuco was quiet now, with a scatter of snow on its forested slopes. Most people I talked to had forgotten the eruption, but down through the forest ran a long thin stream of solidified grey lava, like a scab not yet healed, a classic Andesitic lava flow between levees. This is a comparatively rare occurrence as Andean volcanoes generally have viscous lava which tends to come out more with a bang than a trickle. The forest was bright green right up to the edge of the flow. It all looked very static and permanent and the student I could see hitch-hiking to the emerald lake below had not even been born that day when I had seen that creeping tongue of fire.

'Much closer!' I shouted in the pilot's ear. We whined round the perfect conical peak of Osorno, one of the most beautiful volcanoes in the world, with the icy wind from the open door buffetting our ears. Deep crevasses split the ice-cap, which looked like a blue-tinted meringue. Behind stood the much older relic of the core of another volcano, Puntiagudo, also over 8000 feet high, and as sharp as a claw. The air was clear and Hugh was happy. We flew north across a broken range of volcanoes whose steep slopes were still as forested as the whole of southern Chile had once been. It was a relief to see some stands of the huge Fitzroya, a relative of the redwood, still growing on some of the eastern slopes. There was no sign of tracks or houses. In one place a thin white cascade dropped at least forty metres into a circular bowl of ferns. I doubted whether any white man had ever seen it from the ground. Once again we were over the unknown. Further north a miniature volcano had deposited a splodge of lava on the forest like a ladle of porridge on a green carpet. Then another perfectly circular ash crater had a ski-lift stitched incongruously to its lower slopes.

Villarica volcano was half hidden in its own smoke. The ice on the summit was at least thirty metres thick, sagging downwards to reveal deep blue wrinkles. It looked highly unstable. Steam rolled away from the sharp circular rim spilling over from the fiery throat below. It is one of the most active volcanoes in Chile. There are two towns beneath it: Pucon, and Villarica itself, further away, but still only thirty kilometres from the crater. To consider the future of these towns it is worth recording what happened the last time the volcano had a small erruption in 1971.

At four in the morning of 29 October 1971, skiers who were staying near the volcano were woken by violent explosions in the crater above, which had been totally inactive for at least a year. A small column of steam alternating with black smoke rose in the air.

A month later lava overflowed the crater lip in a narrow stream melting a channel twenty to thirty metres deep in the ice-cap, and descending about 600 metres down the cone. In the centre of the crater an incandescent cone was forming with explosions about every three minutes.

At 23.45 on 29 December the volcano suddenly split open through its summit in a four-kilometre crack along a line roughly NNE–SSW. White-hot lava spewed out, immediately melting the ice-cap and causing six hot mud avalanches which descended the cone at a speed of eighty kilometres an hour (fifty miles per hour) bowling over trees and rocks as large as twenty cubic metres. Three of these avalanches, or lahars as they are technically known, reached Lake Villarica where the two towns are sited. They followed river valleys, and Pucon, though caught between two flows, survived. Two very liquid lava flows then poured down from the ends of the split releasing an estimated thirty million cubic metres of lava. Within twelve hours the eruption decreased again. Fifteen people had died.

Guide books tend to ignore volcanoes and earthquakes. How about this for a description of Latacunga in Ecuador? 'A place where the abundance of light grey lava rock has been artfully employed. Cotopaxi (5,896 metres) is much in evidence, though it is 29 km away.' Latacunga has been destroyed six times by lahars which reach the town about twenty-five minutes after Cotopaxi erupts.

In the Andes lahars are also caused by ice avalanches being dislodged by powerful earthquakes, particularly in the valley between the Cordillera Negra and the Cordillera Blanca in Peru. A horrifying example occurred in 1970 when the town of Yungay was completely buried and 20,000 people lost their lives. One of the most extraordinary properties of these avalanches which may move at very high speeds (480 kilometres per hour at Yungay) is that they become so mixed with air that they become fluidized and travel as if on a cushion of air, which means that they can travel considerable distances *uphill* and easily flow over intervening ridges. They are usually preceded by a blast which causes extensive damage, but much of the material carried down is surprisingly little affected, trees at times do not lose their lichen nor boulders their earth and even people have survived. When I visited Yungay five years after it was destroyed all that was visible of the town were the tops of three palm trees which had been growing in the plaza. Yet high up the mountain the avalanche passed through a valley and the small trees in the bottom were standing as if nothing had happened. Forty million cubic metres of avalanche had flowed over the top!

Another important kind of eruption which could occur at Villarica happened in 1902 when a sustained eruption of Mt Pelée on the island of Martinique in the Caribbean climaxed with dense clouds of incandescent fragments rushing down its slopes (*nuées ardentes*). One of these hit the town of St Pierre with the force of a tornado and the heat of a furnace killing thirty thousand people almost instantly, as it seared the inside of their lungs. Only two people survived, one of them a murderer awaiting execution in a window-less cell. Although Mt Pelée had erupted once fifty years before it had been a very minor affair.

On occasions the magma can actually spill over the rim of a crater in a rock froth. This happens rarely, but the devastation is on a scarcely imaginable scale. The froth (ignimbrite) behaves like a fluidized avalanche and can travel tens of kilometres over flat surfaces, at a speed of 400 kilometres an hour. It then solidifies into a sheet tens of metres thick which may be anything up to 150 kilometres long. Such sheets are very important in the geological structure of the central Andes.

The light white rock that results from these eruptions has been known for centuries. Arequipa, a city in Peru beneath another, young, active volcano El Misti, is built from it, and is famous for the beauty of its architecture. Long may it survive, but on a world list of cities at risk from volcanoes it must stand high. Ignimbrite eruptions, however, are little understood and the word ignimbrite was coined only thirty-five years ago. Fortunately there has only been one such eruption in historical times.

The area around the volcanoes and lakes of south Chile was settled, largely by German immigrants, less than a century ago. They cut down the bamboo thickets and built their wooden farms which look oddly Bavarian beneath the white cones. I had a haircut in a grubby pine-panelled saloon furnished with spittoons and faded mezzotints of World War One aerial dog-fights and Indian princesses crouched by a tropical stream. The ancient arthritic German barber span my chair so that I faced alternately the toothless combs and the dog-fights.

'It's very hot and the tourists have no money,' he said in Spanish, handing me a magazine in German. 'We need another world war, there are too many people.'

I thought of the volcanoes above us.

The Andes, being a young steep range, has many fast-flowing rivers descending steep valleys. The word Andes itself comes from the Peruvian Spanish word 'Andenes' used to describe the terraces which step the mountainsides of the ancient Indian centres of agriculture in order to obtain some level ground. Many of the rivers run chocolate-brown with the sediments scoured from the mountains, but where they run clear with white rapids they are often the home of a remarkable bird, the torrent duck. The Ona Indians, who were extremely observant of wildlife and expert trackers, were full of admiration for the alertness of this duck which always lives in the midst of white water, and its name was given to the most alert of their medicine men. I knew that it was not going to be easy to film, especially as it is still often shot for the pot.

We found a family of these ducks in the river Petrohué in a spectacularly beautiful setting beneath Osorno volcano. During the hot afternoons torrents black with lava dust would pour down the sides of the volcano from the melting ice-cap plunging as black waterfalls into the river.

The torrent ducks feed exclusively on the larva of the stonefly and so they only live in fast rivers with boulders, which cause white water in which the larvae can exist. They seldom fly, and never venture away from the river where they spend most of their time either sleeping on rocks, or hunting for food amongst the weed below the surface with specially adapted, flexible, almost rubber-like bills. They have an astonishing ability to overcome the current, and can make headway against a flow of three metres a second, both over and under the surface. At times the ducks will run across the surface to make their way between eddies, which they are most skilful in exploiting to save energy. The birds have tapered bodies, stiff splayed tails which they use as props on the rocks against the force of the water, large feet, and striking colours. The male has a white head striped with black and a brilliant pinkish-red bill, and the female a grey head and rufous cinnamon breast. It is extraordinary to watch a pair of these brightly coloured birds swimming placidly in an eddy behind a rock while the water piles half a metre high in front of it. To do so for long made me quite giddy on account of the water rushing past.

Most extraordinary of all is the way in which the ducklings are launched into the world from the nest-hole above the rivers. They have been seen to fall eighteen metres onto rocks below, pick themselves up undamaged, and then plunge straight into the white-water rapids. The egg is, in fact, especially large to accommodate their outsized feet, and when they hatch they are already able to emulate their parents in running across the surface of the rapids.

The three days we spent filming them were made miserable by innumerable large tabanid horse-flies. They were black and orange, furry, and the size of bumble bees, and if given the opportunity sucked one's blood. They were particularly attracted to brown sweaters or blue jeans. They were clumsy fliers but their sheer quantity was enough to drive us a little crazy as we were trying to keep still to observe the ducks. Mercifully they kept out of the stuffy darkness of Hugh's hide, but Donaldo one day killed 137 in half an hour, chopping them in half with his sheath knife as they settled on his wrist. Nobody knows where they go at night or any details of their life-cycles. After the first heavy shower of rain they all vanished.

On the mainland of Chile one of my principal advisors was Luis Peña. Lucho, as he was always known to us, is an entomologist. But he is an unusual entomologist in that his interests spread far beyond his speciality – tenebrionid beetles – and indeed far beyond the insect world. Since he was a young man he has accompanied and helped zoological expeditions of all kinds which have visited Chile. Chileans, on the whole, travel very little in their own country but Lucho knew it well and had an encyclopaedic enthusiasm for everything from flies to gold mines.

While I had been in Chiloé, my assistant producer Keenan Smart had been working with Lucho and another specialist cameraman Rodger Jackman at one of Lucho's favourite haunts on the coast near Osorno. This was 450 miles north of the San Rafael forest, but although warmer and somewhat drier it was basically the same kind of wet 'Valdivian' forest. Rodger Jackman had already filmed Darwin's frog *Rhinoderma* and the extraordinary way in which the males appear to eat the developing eggs, which are taken into an unusually large vocal sac until they are large enough to jump out of the adult's mouth, for David Attenborough's series *Life on Earth*. I wanted film of the defence technique of that most ingenious frog, *Rhinoderma*, in which it will leap into water, going into a rigid catatonic state, and float away on its back with a brightly coloured belly visible, camouflaged to blend with the dead leaves of nothofagus beech. Rodger's speciality is photography of insects, small mammals, etc., and there were a variety of other forest creatures which I wanted him to film. The difficulty was to catch them and keep them alive.

When Keenan and I had been on a recce with Lucho, a problem became apparent. Lucho's standard method of collection was designed to obtain specimens for museums. He was extremely adept in catching insects but they all ended up skewered on pins – unbelievably large numbers of them: Lucho once, I was told, sold a collection of 40,000 flies to a museum in São Paulo, Brazil. (What anyone would do with 40,000 flies in São Paulo is a different matter.) The first time that we thought we might have trouble was when we caught a number of lizards. These, Lucho assured us, would do fine in plastic bags. It was not until we were sitting down to supper in Lucho's camper van with the rain pouring down outside that I noticed a lizard climbing up the curtains. Every single one of them had escaped. We had similar problems with the large and spectacular spiders. They would be thrust into plastic bags with enthusiasm, to be taken out later sadly bent and legless. I had last seen Lucho and Keenan trying to catch *Rhyncolestes*, the rarest mammal in Chile, a rat opossum.

In 1493 when the navigator Pinzon returned to Spain after sailing to the West Indies with Christopher Columbus on his epic voyage of discovery, he presented to the Spanish monarchs, Ferdinand and Isabella, a furry animal the size of a rabbit which had a long tail which it could curl round a branch to support itself, and, stranger still, a pouch on its abdomen furnished with an odd number of teats on which were suckling diminutive young. It was the first marsupial (a common opossum) to be seen in Europe. Until then all known mammals – animals which have hair and milk-producing glands – developed their young in a womb or uterus, connected for nourishment to a placenta or afterbirth. Opossums had only one outlet from the body, like birds, and it was many years before it was discovered that the female's egg cells are fertilised internally but are 'born' only about twelve days later in such an undeveloped state that many features of the body are undifferentiated. On rudimentary limbs they haul themselves to the pouch or marsupium where they fasten onto a nipple and continue their development.

There are still some seventy-five species of opossum living in South America, a good example of the 'radiation' of variations on a basic kind of animal if there are opportunities in different habitats. The rarest of all is the Chilean rat opossum which was discovered in the 1920s and is known only from four specimens. I had seen one of these in the Natural History Museum in Santiago: a scientist produced from a drawer a small flat skin on a cardboard stretcher with cotton-wool popping through its eye sockets. It was difficult to feel excited about it. In life, it is a long-nosed, sharp toothed, rather shrew-like little animal with a short tail that runs along fallen tree-trunks in thick forests and lives on insects and worms. It is an animal with relatives in the high forests of Ecuador and Colombia and it belongs to a very ancient branch of the marsupial family tree (the Caenolestids).

Keenan and Lucho tried trapping for a week at Osorno where the animal had been caught in 1943, but with no success. However, they did obtain a female and young of the other family of marsupials, the Didelphids: a 'monito del monte', *Dromiciops australis*, which if less interesting to scientists, was much prettier to photograph with its big bulging black eyes and furry young.

The forest held other surprises. We soon became used to the attentions of a black leech which would fasten on our ankles to suck our blood (as did the fleas that infested the hotel) but Lucho told us that there was also a giant black leech fifty centimetres long, *Americobdella valdiviana*. Unfortunately the fine weather, which had blessed our filming, had made the forest exceptionally dry, and our promises of handsome rewards to the local population produced instead a smaller (thirty-five centimetres) bright orange leech of singularly repulsive appearance. This was duly filmed, and since Lucho had a remarkable facility for discovering new species – only that week he had found a new buprestid beetle – we planned its triumphant presentation to the British Museum.

Alas it did not survive the rigours of life in Lucho's camper, and Keenan discovered it one day in a paper bag in the larder in an advanced state of putrefaction. He buried it forthwith, but when Lucho found out he was heartbroken.

We had spent some time trying to get the leech to feed on ourselves, or frogs, which were numerous in the forest; only later did I learn that it probably ate worms.

The dangers of Lucho's chaotic larder threatened to be more serious. He was, it appeared to us, astonishingly casual in his handling of the cyanide for his killing-bottles, and Keenan was more than a little worried that it would end up in the sandwiches.

And yet there were more subtle dangers. One day, by the side of a river, Lucho pointed out to me a rather ordinary-looking tree which had pendulous bell-shaped flowers, the colour of, but slightly smaller than, a foxglove bell. He told me that ten years before a local man had been sent to collect a branch of this tree for an American scientist. As he rode back across the mountain carrying the branch over his shoulder he went mad and remains mad to this day. It was the sorcerer's tree (*Latua pubiflora*) which belongs to the nightshade family, and was used by the Mapuche Indians of the Valdivia area to cause delirium and insanity. There are more than ninety species of plants used by the Indians of the Americas for their intoxicating properties, and it is no exaggeration to say that whole cultures were enslaved by them.

Before Lucho told me his story I had always enjoyed my ramblings through this strange forest. Afterwards it never seemed quite the same.

5

The Monkey-Puzzle Forest, Condors and Central Chile

At Puerto Montt the Pan American Highway begins, which, with the exception of a short distance in the Darien jungles of Panama and Colombia, runs the whole remaining length of the two continents. It is a busy road, and is mostly paved. We got to know that road well, as any journey into the Andes meant first heading north or south along the 'Panamericana'.

As we headed north from Puerto Montt the road lay between the blackened stumps of what was once one of the finest forests in the world – of the alerce (*Fitzroya cupressoides*), a relative of the giant sequoia of California. This magnificent tree grows extremely slowly attaining a diameter of ten centimetres after sixty years, and only sets seed after several centuries. It is an evergreen and reaches a height of forty metres, living for two thousand years. It makes a very durable and well-figured timber and in consequence the tree has been almost eradicated. Although it is now protected by law, it is illegal only to cut down an alerce, not to sell its timber. So the moment a tree is cut down it becomes legal, a nonsensical situation which leaves plenty of opportunities for unscrupulous logging. So slow is its rate of growth it is unlikely that the tree can ever be re-established, so the protection of the few stands that remain is paramount.

Another tree native to the area, and restricted to a narrow zone of Chile and Argentina about 200 miles long, is the monkey-puzzle, or araucarian pine. This tree, which takes its name from the curious branches ringed with close-packed scaly helices of spiny leaves, was such a favourite with Victorian nurserymen that I sometimes wonder whether there are not more of them growing in British gardens than in the Andes. This tree was also threatened by indiscriminate logging, but since there are now forest reserves, and since it grows much more quickly and sets very large quantities of seed, its future is far less precarious. It is an ancient form of tree, and its seeds, released from strange globular cones on the ends of the branches of the female tree, were an important part of the diet of the Indian tribes nearby. Some ornithologists believe that the slender-billed parakeet, which is exclusive to Chile, developed its unusually straight and slender beak to break open the cones and probe between the spikey leaves of the

63

araucaria. Lucho also assured us that there were some seventy species of insect that lived on the araucaria and nowhere else.

The araucarian forest has a fairly open floor and it is easy to walk through, but the over-all impression of these strange trees is so bizarre that it is hard not to believe that one is walking through a Hollywood set for *The Lost World* with a dinosaur round the next corner. The snow-capped volcanoes framed by the dome-shaped pines, their green branches like giant curved-up catkins, is one of the most memorable sights of the Andes.

Amidst the calm beauty of this forest it comes as a shock to be suddenly confronted by a wall of lava as high as a house, even when it is cold and inert. One of the most active volcanoes in Chile is Llaima, and an eruption in 1957 destroyed a large area of monkey-puzzle forest. The Andesitic lavas of these volcanoes are very viscous and move slowly, cooling as they descend the slope of the mountain until they are advancing only a few metres a day. The edges of the flow cool too and form natural banks or levées which channel the lava in a certain direction, raising the flow five or even ten metres above the level of the ground. The front of a flow may be considerably higher where the lava has cooled and piled up on itself. One in the north of Chile is 500 metres high.

On the slopes of Llaima the lava had channelled itself around one small patch of forest to leave it growing like an island of green in the midst of a sterile brown sea. The trees on the edge had been scorched to white skeletons, but those in the centre lived, and a red-backed hawk had nested in one of them.

There are volcanoes in the Andes not only in every stage of growth, but also of decay. The stumps and cones are scattered through the folded landscape with the new cones piled on top. But it is the active ones that impress. One cannot stand next to one without being struck by the immense quantity of matter that has been ejected from the centre of the earth and by the power of the slow unstoppable flow of lava.

So far we had not been able to film a volcano in eruption, so our next stop as we worked our way north was at Chillán. Here we saw a lava flow from 1945 filling a whole valley floor. There the forest might never have existed, yet at either side it had regrown right to the edge of the lava, the burnt trees replaced by new growth. The lava was different here: a coarse type of black obsidian – volcanic glass. It had heaved and split into huge ridges of boulders that had cleft as they cooled into curved-faceted glassy rocks with sharp edges. Those edges were always waiting for a false move.

I was struck by the similarity of the glaciers of the south to the lava flows of this temperate region; a comparison not as strange as it appears at first. The front of each is forced on by the weight of matter behind. The ice gouges rock to form deep valleys, and then retreats to leave fiords and fertile boulder clay. The lava flows down valleys cutting down the vegetation, but weathers down to a fertile soil. In this valley both had been at work. The ice had cut the rock like a knife, the lava filled the wound. To see the lava piled against the forest is like the illusion of the negative of a glacier. Black for white, hot for cold, rock for water.

PREVIOUS PAGE   Chillán volcano

OPPOSITE   Temperate rain-forest near the glacier
INSET   Coicopihue

ABOVE   San Rafael glacier. The face is 60 metres high

OVERLEAF   Villarica volcano

26

1957 lava flow
from Llaima volcano
BELOW
Cerro Puntiagudo with
Monte Tronador behind

OPPOSITE TOP
Giant leech
CENTRE
Marsupial mouse
BOTTOM
Torrent ducks

OVERLEAF
Llaima volcano and
monkey-puzzle forest

OPPOSITE
Giant humming-bird
INSET
Detail of cactus
of Chilean savanna

LEFT
Chinchilla
BELOW
Cactus of
Chilean savanna

PREVIOUS PAGE
Atacama desert coast

Grey gulls
INSET Grey gull shades
chicks in desert

OVERLEAF Male condor
flying over the desert
INSET A mature male
dominates immature
birds and females
feeding on a carcass

37/38

The curves and shining surfaces of the obsidian had an aesthetic fascination. There is a simple joy in finding beauty where no eye has focussed before. And like the soft curves of wind-eroded granite in the desert, these had a complex purity of natural form. And what a setting, when the volcano above pouts a soft feather of white smoke high into the air and growls in a voice of grinding boulders.

We camped in a refuge below the volcano, and that night watched the plume glow red from the fire beneath and a burst of red tracery as glowing boulders were exploded into the air. I was excited, but apprehensive, about climbing it in the morning. Hugh had returned to England, so Rodger was to accompany me to do the filming. We had been told that the volcano did not have a crater and that the eruptions were out of fissures and vents between the loose rocks of the summit. I decided that the best view for filming would be from the older summit, about half a kilometre south-east of the new cone. We set off up the sliding slopes of pumice.

Since the whole side of a volcano consists of matter that has slid down from the top, it is inevitably unstable, and slides at every step. We had to pick a way where each step would not start a minor landslide. It was hard work and soon my calf muscles were protesting. I had been timing the eruptions. The big ones seemed to be coming about every forty minutes but others varied with ten or twenty minutes between them. I could not establish a pattern. I avoided the snow fields which looked, and probably were, easy going because I had been warned by an experienced mountaineer never to go on snow on a mountain without being roped up for protection against crevasses, avalanches and sliding.

After a stiff climb we reached some fumaroles where steam wafted from sulphur-stained rock that was warm to the touch. Scarcely had the camera been set up when there was an eruption.

It began with a crumph and then a billowing mushroom of white smoke and steam shot up like an atom-bomb blast. A second later came the noise, like several jumbo-jets taking off together. The same rumbling roar was underlain by a siren-like whine as if the volcano had a reed in its throat. We were just getting used to this dramatic spectacle, which seemed very close, when there was another even louder whoomph, and this time a billow of black smoke went up on the side away from us. A large shower of red-hot rocks were thrown hundreds of feet into the air.

'Hey, do you think we are all right?' shouted Rodger, still filming.

I watched the eruption very closely to see if any bits were coming our way. Fortunately they did not. 'We're O.K.,' I said, thinking that if it got worse there was precious little that we could do about it.

'My knees are knocking!'

'Don't shake the camera!'

Rodger went on filming as the black and white plumes towered and mingled and finally died. He looked quite shaken when he stood back from the tripod.

'I've never been so scared before,' he said.

We were both delighted though, at having the luck to film the blast.

Now we were joined by Keenan and Donaldo, and set off again, taking turns with the knapsacks and tripod. The cloud that had been forecast by the locals for mid-day began to blow round us, and I took a bearing on the top of the road below. It is very easy to come down the wrong side of a volcano, where everything looks the same. But the wind was so strong that I thought we might well find a clear patch in which to film another eruption. Coming over a final ridge we were on the lip of a crater about 500 metres across. A smooth inverted cone dropped away beneath us to an impressive depth. We were now at an altitude of 10,500 feet. Out of the wind, in the lee of the crater where it was warm again, we rested and all felt an overpowering desire to go to sleep. In fact all the others did, not a sensible thing to do when a wind shift of only a few degrees could envelop us in poisonous gas from the erupting crater. I woke them with some difficulty. Then there was another eruption. We were now on a level with the erupting summit, and the noise was the more impressive as we were surrounded in cloud, and could see nothing.

It began to rain and as the drops hit the crater wall around us it began to steam. Until then, despite the fumaroles, we had not realised how hot it was. I decided to wait for another half hour in the hope that the clouds would break. They did and the volcano spoke again. We got the shot.

As we began to descend it started to hail. At first it was just a nuisance, but the storm got heavier and heavier, the thunder-claps were getting nearer, drowning the noises of the crater, and the hail whitened the lava slopes. We started to hurry. Going down loose pumice is easy; it absorbs a lot of energy and one can run with loping strides, sliding and sinking with each step. By the time we had gone down about a thousand feet the hail was really hard, rattling on our helmets and stinging our hands. We were grateful to reach our jeep without incident.

The municipality were spending millions of dollars constructing a ski-lift up Chillán. I thought they were optimists.

In a series to be called *The Flight of the Condor* I naturally needed good footage of condors flying. I was very pleased with what Hugh had filmed in the Paine, but I also wanted to investigate the possibility of filming them from the air. I knew that they were frightened by the sound of the engine of a plane or helicopter so I decided to try to approach one in a glider. Gliders had been used to study vultures in Africa so it seemed worth a try. I soon met an instructor at the Santiago gliding club who said that he had already flown with condors many times.

We dropped our tow at 3000 feet above sea level and picked up lift almost immediately close to the western slopes of the escarpment north of Santiago. I was immediately surprised how close we flew to the mountain, almost parting the bushes with the long white wings of our modern German sailplane as we began to spiral tightly round and round in bumpy air. Gliding in the Andes is rather different to gliding on the South Downs and there in the middle of the afternoon on a hot day the conditions can only be described as extreme.

At first I thought it was splendid to be soaring in the mountains like a condor and was thrilled when the dry foothills dropped away beneath us and the white peaks began to show beyond. But after the first half-hour, when we had successfully doubled our altitude and had soared north-east to a new ridge, I was beginning to enjoy the surroundings less and be more aware of the turbulence inside me. I had taken the precaution of having little lunch, but had wined and dined too well the night before. A lot had happened since then, including a marked earth tremor in the middle of the night, but my stomach remembered. We swept up to a crescent-shaped cliff marked as 6000 feet high on my map. The surface, I saw, was flecked with the white splashes of guano below the roosts of eagles or condors. Then we hit an almighty updraught. The climb meter stuck to the maximum rate of ascent of five metres a second and before I had time for another look the cliff was far below. We went up at over eight metres a second for a minute and a half and as we bumped in and out of the lift the white wings bent like feathers. I noticed that there was space for the pilot and passenger to wear parachutes and I began to realise why – but we didn't have any. For a moment I noticed a black-chested buzzard eagle sharing the same air current, then we whirled in opposite directions.

I shut my eyes for a while to eliminate the confusion of a constantly circling horizon. We were now over 10,000 feet high. I had had great plans of taking photos and dictating my impressions into a tape-recorder. Instead I tried to sleep.

At 110 kms per hour we slid towards the next massive row of peaks, and yet more turbulence, yet more circling. Would the horizon never be still? I was in a cold sweat brought on partly by the altitude, partly by circling constantly from hot sun into cold shadow, but mostly by acute airsickness. I buried my face in a plastic bag. We were horribly near the rocks again and I wondered how on earth we would get out of these valleys if we lost the lift. We gyrated for a while over the ski resort of Farellones and headed south across another ridge.

Suddenly I saw a condor right ahead. My first reaction was that it was odd to look down on a condor. I just had time to notice the sun gleaming on the white secondary feathers, and see that the bird too was being tossed about in the air currents when again I had to put my face in my bag. What a splendid romantic idea to go soaring in the Andes – and what an outcome!

The condor drifted down below us and swooped up to perch in a crevice. We span down, and with my stomach lurching, skimmed a wingtip past the rock. I could not see into the opening. I realised that this was a hopeless method for filming. The pilot had to concentrate too much on staying in the air.

We landed after two hours and twenty minutes, having flown at least 150 kilometres in a straight line but many many more in circles. I had shared the air-currents of the Andes with a condor but I felt as weak as if I had a fever.

In Scotland, locals call the buzzard 'the tourists' eagle', and in the Andes eagles are frequently mistaken for condors. But anyone who has once seen a condor in flight is unlikely to confuse it with anything else. The broad straight wings with their spreading 'fingers', the heavy wedge of a tail and the short neck all add up to a characteristic silhouette. Its wing area is nearly two square metres, and with a weight of about twelve kilos this gives it the low wing-loading necessary for slow soaring flight. One can watch a condor fly for hours without seeing it flap, and then it is usually only to aid take-off, or a few strokes before gliding again. I have only once seen a group of condors flapping hard, and that was as they raced downwind across the Peruvian highlands ahead of a storm. In the air the bird moves with such skill and grace that one forgets how ugly and cumbersome it is on the ground. It is also hard to get an accurate impression of its size. The first time that I realised just how big a condor is, was when I saw a stuffed one perched on the grand piano of the Director of the Chilean Academy of Music. It dwarfed the instrument.

Condors are birds of the vast solitudes of the mountains, shying away from areas frequented by man. There are a few in Colombia, but they are mostly to be found from Ecuador south to Cape Horn. They do not fly north of the Rio Negro, on the coastal plains of Argentina, which forms the northern boundary of Patagonia, nor do they fly to the coast in Ecuador or Colombia. But they do frequent the desert coast of Peru in the summer.

Condors have been kept in captivity until over fifty years old, but nobody knows their natural life-span. It must be great, however, as the young do not change to their full breeding plumage with white neck ring and a large patch of white on the upper surface of the wings until they are eight years old (before that they are brown). They are social birds inasmuch as the young fly with the adults for several years after they have fledged, and they observe a pecking-order when feeding together on the ground, established by making a nibbling beak to beak action. It is likely that they find their prey entirely by keen eye-sight, watching each other, as well as the ground, as they cruise in wide circles over the mountains. When one condor sees carrion, or the activities of caracara carrion-hawk or turkey-vulture, it descends and the others follow it down.

It has been suggested that flying along ridges using hill-lift from a strong wind is also a good way to pick up the scent of carrion, but it appears that the condor has little sense of smell. Darwin conducted some basic experiments, carrying a piece of meat wrapped in white paper past a row of tethered condors at a distance of three yards. 'But no notice whatever was taken. I then threw it on the ground within one yard of an old male bird; he looked at it for a moment with attention, but then regarded it no more. With a stick I pushed it closer and closer, until at last he touched it with his beak; the paper was then instantly torn off with fury, and at the same moment every bird in the long row began struggling and flapping its wings.'

Since then there have been many more scientific experiments on birds' sense of smell and it is now known that turkey-vultures and yellow-headed vultures *can* smell. There is little doubt that the condor – an intelligent adaptable bird – exploits the turkey-vulture's talents when it can.

Condors belong to the family Cathartidae, the New World vultures, though there is some argument that they may be related to storks. They have extremely powerful short hooked bills for ripping flesh, but their feet are normally used for walking and bracing against the ripping force of their bill, and do not have the strength of an eagle's talons. However, condors frequently perch on trees so the feet do have some strength. Scientists are disinclined to believe tales of condors flying off with prey – the Indians of Peru believe that they will steal babies – but Sr Galo Plaza, a former President of Ecuador, assured me that a free-ranging pet condor which had been owned by his sister had to be shot because it started to kill young animals. 'And one day it flew back with a lamb.' We heard other similar accounts.

A condor approaches its prey with great circumspection, usually landing some distance uphill, and walking towards it in an ungainly manner. With the wings folded the whitish secondaries form a ring and give the birds an odd look of old ladies in bonnets and full stiff skirts. Close-to, the head and neck, devoid of feathers, can only be described as hideous. Both sexes have a smart white collar, and the male has a short comb the same purplish-to-black colour as the head and neck. Adults go to considerable effort to keep clean, wiping their heads and necks on grass or sand after feeding, but the young in the nest have a disagreeable habit of defecating down their legs to keep cool by evaporation.

Darwin was told that condors could live for five or six weeks without feeding, and they are known to gorge themselves when they have the chance. I was told of one eating an eight-kilo piece of liver at one sitting – two thirds of its own weight. A heavily gorged condor will be unable to take off on the level and will often walk some hundreds of metres uphill to save the effort of flapping. The Indians and Spaniards used to take advantage of this clumsiness to catch them, by putting bait in a circular enclosure where the unfed birds could land, but after eating could not take off. Even now it is not unusual to see up to forty condors on a dead horse or other large animal, in areas as far apart as the equator and Patagonia. In Chile they are now shot less and their numbers are increasing, but in much of central Peru, where there is a large Indian population, they are scarce.

Condors have figured in Indian mythology in South America for thousands of years. There is the unmistakable outline of one drawn on the famous pampa of the Nazca lines, and their image appears on the pottery and textiles of many of the early pre-Inca cultures. They are part of the coat-of-arms of four of the South American republics and Bolivia's highest order of merit is the Order of the Condor. Considering the bird is a vulture I find this choice rather odd.

The Indians of the highlands eat condor flesh, use the wing bones for flutes, roast and eat the eyes to sharpen their sight, and use other parts of the anatomy for a variety of cures. The quills make cigarette-holders. I was assured by one farmer that it was no good shooting a condor as it flew towards you, for even a rifle bullet would be deflected by the feathers. You had to shoot them from behind. This impregnability is not borne out in practise. The guards of the Peruvian guano-bird colonies used to shoot as many as fifty condors a year during the short nesting season in the mistaken belief that the birds upset the breeding and thus the supply of guano.

Condors also figure in Quechua mythology. The Quechua were the subjects of the Incas, whose empire at its widest stretched from central Chile to the equator, some three thousand miles. Quechua, Roman Catholic and Republican Peruvian calendars have by now been inextricably interwoven and the ancient festivals debased to mere orgies of drinking and dancing, but in a few of the villages around Cusco, such as Paruro and Cotabambas, a strange contest takes place which is said to symbolise the struggle between Indian and Conquistador. A condor is caught and its feet are sewn to the shoulders of a bull with leather thongs passed under the bull's hide. The two maddened animals then career around the plaza until the bull wearies, and if the condor survives it is released the following morning. Bulls and bull-fighting were introduced from Spain and the triumph of the condor is said to symbolise the successful resistance of the Indians.

At the northern end of the Callejón de Huaylas, the deep valley in Peru between the Cordilleras Blanca and Negra, several villages hold another even more brutal 'fiesta': the *Condorachi* (the tearing of the condor). The bird is suspended either by its wings or its feet from a rope in an archway and the mounted villagers strike at it with their fists as they ride underneath. The man who delivers the fatal blow then bites out the long yellow tongue of the bird and earns himself the honour of paying for the next fiesta. It is worth noting that this contest is not as one-sided as it sounds. Wounds from a condor's beak or talons are notorious for their liability to infection, because they are implanted with the bacteria that flourish in rotten meat, and many of the horsemen are slashed on their hands and faces. What is more, this ritual slaughter probably has far less effect on the population of condors in Peru than the more educated Peruvian's love of random shooting.

I soon came to know the location of various condor's nests, but could not find one that was filmable. They all tended to be on convex cliff faces which might be as much as three thousand feet high. I needed a nest which was overlooked by a viewpoint about thirty metres away, so that we could set up a hide to film the adult birds bringing in food to their young. This is very different from dangling on the end of a rope to take a snapshot of a chick looking scared, though I had great difficulty explaining this to the local country people.

Nineteen years before, I had ridden into the mountains to visit a condor's nest and I remembered climbing down into it and seeing a large single white egg.

I had written to the owner of the farm where I had seen the condor's egg, and one day I was excited to get a reply. He had sold that farm but now had a smaller one nearby at Chincolco about three hours north of Santiago. Distances in South America are usually measured in hours by road on the basis that the roads are so variable that a measurement in kilometres is not much help to anybody. I arranged to drive up one weekend.

When I first met Julio Prado I had been struck by his energy and the work involved in making a success of a new farm, rearing Hereford cattle on the desperately dry foothills of the Andes. It was extraordinary now how he and his charming wife Ines both remembered the details of that visit nineteen years before. Even more extraordinary was the fact that Ines now had ten children, including several extremely pretty daughters who were at university. Their sons had mostly followed their father into veterinary medicine.

As a young man, Julio had got to know the neighbouring mountains very well. He had climbed most of the neighbouring peaks, and each year, until the recent frontier disputes had prevented it, he and his family had ridden over the mountains into Argentina.

The Andes of central Chile are roughly 200 miles wide at a height of 4800 feet. (Snowdon is under 3600 feet). It is an area so little known, even next to Santiago, a city of nearly four million inhabitants, that a large American transport jet carrying service personnel and their families was recently lost there and never found. In the same region a Uruguayan football team crashed and were forced to turn cannibal before they were rescued. In the summer nomadic goat-herds follow their flocks into the alpine pastures, but when the first gales of winter bring the snow the range is deserted. Julio's old farm was on the edge of this arid wilderness. He described to me how on one occasion he had seen what he estimated to be 250 condors feeding on the carcass of a cow. Unable to take off because of the amount they had eaten, he had seen them disgorge before taking flight. Three times he had watched condors attack and kill young calves, which were particularly vulnerable when the year was dry and the pasture bare. He claimed that the condors used to take ninety percent of the calves then, and he had watched a mother cow standing over her calf protecting it and butting at the condor which continued to harrass her until she stepped on the calf and injured it, when the condor got its way. He said that with the first peck the condor would disembowel the calf and then go for the eyes and the tongue. They would also wait until the cows had to go down to the streams to drink, leaving their calves unprotected. Once with Ines he watched condors attack a group of goats that had kids. They cornered the goats against a junction of two fences and then killed the kids. Ines fully supported this account of the drama, which they had witnessed from the opposite side of a valley where they could do nothing to intervene.

On the other hand, Julio had never seen a condor attack a man, and even when he had taken young condors from the nest, which he had done several times for the zoo in Santiago, he was never attacked although the male came to have a close look only a few metres above.

Julio knew of three nests on his old property. One of them was only accessible by being lowered on three lassos tied end to end, but I could certainly go to look at the two others. One of them had been in use since his grandfather's day in 1906.

One of Julio's sons went on ahead with horses up to their former farm at Pedernal and the next morning we set off to ride to the first nest. Julio believes that given the opportunity the condor nests quite low down in the Andes and that it is only the pressure of Man that has driven it back into the heights. I was surprised how accessible this nest was. It was about two hours' ride uphill through scrub and cactus, and was in a shallow cave-like hollow on the side of a low cliff. Julio had at different times caught two condors here for the zoo, but we soon saw that it was deserted. Instead, a black-chested buzzard eagle had built its nest there, an untidy pile of sticks on a jutting pedestal of rock. It was a great disappointment that there was no trace of a condor, as the site would have been very good to film.

The next day we rode to the second nest, another three hours on an alarming track that skirted a steep valley. This nest was unknown to the employee who led us there and it was an odd experience for me to have to lead the way on the scraps of memory from nineteen years before. Alas, there was neither egg nor chick, but there was a lot of whitewash from droppings about and the bare patch of rock where the nest had been was still clean. I picked up a condor's feather which had had all its barbules removed by the chick pecking at it. Two adult condors and an immature one flew close-by inspecting me as I climbed back up. Further down the cliff – which was accessible only from the top – was another perch splashed with white which appeared to be a roost. It was not an ideal place to film, as the only possible hide position was about twelve feet from the nest and we would have had to use a remote-controlled camera. But after a whole year of asking up and down the Andes this was the best chance we had come up with yet. It seemed crazy that I of all people should be the one to know an accessible nest-site. By now, Julio's son Gonzalo had become caught up in the enthusiasm of the chase and he promised to let me know if the condors laid again.

Condors usually lay only one egg. Incubation lasts two months, and the chick remains in the nest – no more than a bare scrape on the floor of a shallow cave – for six months. As the juvenile is dependent on the adults for some time for food, condors only nest every two years. This made our searches even more difficult, but I hoped the Pedernal nest might be used the following year.

One story which had recurred several times was how condors would drive animals over precipices to kill them. One day in the Paine park I saw a large lamb on a distant cliff ledge, and I at once noticed that there were condors perched nearby. There were fourteen altogether. Two were below the foot of the small cliff on which the animal was apparently cornered, one was perched half way up, and another strategically placed at the only way out for the lamb. Other condors watched on the skyline, apparently waiting for the feast.

I waited but my presence disturbed the condors, which took off. I drove off thinking I had probably saved the lamb.

When I went back again the next day I came to the conclusion that I had misinterpreted the whole thing. I climbed up to the ledge and found that it was over a metre wide with some grazing on it. The condors were still perched nearby, with no sign of the lamb alive or dead. It was really a young sheep and no condor could have lifted it. I decided that this was simply a favourite roost for the condors in the strength of wind that had been blowing the last two days. The sheep might have been scared off the cliff by a condor suddenly flying low overhead – one certainly gave me enough of a fright. But that second day it all looked much less likely. The same controversy exists about whether golden eagles will drive red deer to their deaths in Scotland. Some claim to have seen it, others that it is impossible.

North of Santiago the valley which runs north to south down Chile is cut into a series of river basins by 'curtain ranges' of mountains that run from the Andes to the sea. The cultivated land is in these basins and the hills have an increasingly dry vegetation of acacia and cactus and puyas – relatives of the pineapple. These mountains were once the home of the chinchilla, a delightful furry animal like a rabbit kitten with a curly fluffy tail. In 1899 Chile exported half a million chinchilla skins to be converted into fur coats. By 1907 the number had fallen to 28,000 valued at up to $500 per dozen. By 1920 they were so scarce that it took three years to find a dozen animals from which most commercially bred chinchillas are now descended. One species (*brevicaucata*) has disappeared, but I find it difficult to believe that an animal which can breed up to a height of 21,000 feet can have vanished from the whole vast range of the Andes.

There is a secret site a few hours north of Santiago where CONAF are protecting a population of the *Chinchilla laniger*. (The local inhabitants are very reluctant to reveal where chinchillas live. Like goldminers, they do not like to tell you where their gold comes from.)

It looked like good cowboy country: towering cactus and scrub so dry that it looked dead. It was extremely hot. Night was coming on fast as I drove up a track with a CONAF guide. We scrambled up a scree slope, making, I thought, far too much noise for shy animals. We waited in silence for an hour and a half as the moon rose. It was deathly quiet. We saw nothing, and I was bitten all over the backside by vinchucas, an unpleasant blood-sucking insect (*Triatoma infestans*) that carries Chargas disease which gave Darwin the symptoms that disabled his latter years.

In the morning we climbed fast to the top of a mountain in the blazing heat. I had never before been so conscious of the sweat running down behind my ears into my collar. It was difficult not to slip on the scree and become impaled on the cactus.

There were plenty of traces of chinchillas about, small black droppings and the dusty scrapes where they roll to condition their fur. I was fascinated to watch the vinchuca bugs come creeping out of their crevices towards us as soon as we sat on the rocks. How they knew we were there I don't know, but they had a very efficient location system, and they must make life miserable for the chinchillas. I chose a couple of sites to build dummy hides out of dead cactus and sacking to get the chinchillas used to odd shapes on their territory. They have the reputation of being extremely wary, with very acute senses, especially hearing. They were not going to be easy to film. We would have to use an electronic image-intensifier which works like an army night-sight for a rifle, where a faint image is scanned by a television camera and multiplied onto a screen which the camera films. The only time there would be enough light would be with the full moon.

This time my cameraman was Jim Saunders. We left him in his hide in the moonlight liberally supplied with insecticide, and watched the magnificent spectacle of the full moon rising over the semi-desert mountains. Three nights running we took the equipment up using a mule and the warden's mare.

On the third night Jim got one shot of one chinchilla which then bolted at the faint electronic whine of the image-intensifier. It was almost certainly the first time a chinchilla had been filmed in the wild but it was a poor return for two days on the road and three nights filming, and we were unlikely to get more. Luckily I had arranged for an enclosure to be built on the side of a mountain into which we released some captive chinchillas which could be filmed as if in the wild. This is a technique frequently used in making natural history films, but one that we had to resort to very little.

6

The Humboldt Current and the Atacama Desert

It is impossible to live for any length of time beneath the shadow of the Andes without being conscious of the tremendous physical barrier they represent. There are said to be seventy-five peaks above 20,000 feet and 2000 over 16,000 feet. In the Rocky Mountains a 14,000 foot peak is considered very impressive, whilst in Bolivia I have driven a Land Rover to 18,500 feet.

The greatest of these magnificent mountains is Aconcagua, which towers above its neighbours a short distance to the north of Santiago. It is the highest mountain in the Americas, or the western hemisphere, and at 23,034 feet it is only exceeded by peaks in the Himalayas, Tibet, and the Karakoram. It was long thought to be a volcano, indeed Darwin noted reports that it had erupted, but recent geological surveys have shown that it is folded sedimentary rock, the highest knuckle of the western edge of the continent where it crumples against the thrust of the Nazca plate.

The effect of this great wall of mountains on the land beneath is dramatic. For 3500 kilometres between the Pacific and the Andes stretches one of the driest deserts in the world: the Atacama Desert.

In the popular imagination a desert is a plain covered with huge sand dunes, while geographers are inclined to call areas of dry cactus and scrub desert too. The Atacama merges into savannah at either end, but in the centre it is a mountainous area, totally bankrupt biologically. In places the classic crescent Barkhan dunes crawl over the surface at about four metres a year; in others the surface is of sun-darkened rock. At the coast, which has few openings for ports, the land has risen in stages above the sea in a series of terraces, and it remains sterile to the distant heights of the mountains, where at last the air becomes cool enough to condense moisture as snow-storms on the white peaks of the Cordillera.

The first time I drove up the highway that threads this vast solitude it was unpaved, and I shall never forget the dust and the torture of those thousands of kilometres of corrugated road. Now it is a black strip of asphalt drawn across a landscape as naked as the surface of the moon. It is surprising what a difference that imprint of civilisation makes, an umbilicus which promises the safety and comfort of the city even though it may be hundreds of miles to the next settlement. But it is still hard to drive through that emptiness, where not even vultures fly, without apprehension. It is at its loneliest in northern Chile where it runs, straight as a bullet, along immense intermontane plains. The scenery of dry mountains is magnificent, but there is absolutely no foreground to provide variety and interest and driving for hour after hour at a steady 120 kilometres per hour induces a state of torpor that we found could only be aleviated by listening to cassette music (one is far out of range of radio stations). We had a wide choice from Elton John to Mozart, and it was odd how one could select a mood and a music to fit the slowly moving pattern of dry hills. Every once in a while a solitary green bush or tree would wave its leaves beside the tarmac in place of the usual crucifix: each recording a sudden death. Watered by passing travellers, they were desperately fragile monuments to Man's transience. Sometimes, especially in southern Peru where the road skirts the coast looping along the cliffs, we would encounter a forest of iron crosses where a major disaster had occurred. Once there was a shrine where a busload of Ecuadorian students had met their end in Chile; another where a returning victorious football team had gone over a cliff.

In the afternoon the wind blew across the desert from the coast with the breath of a dragon. We would block the windows with paper to keep out the sun, and our fingers were burnt on the steering-wheel. We passed through a landscape with all the features of erosion by water – complex drainage systems, gravel plains – yet it was as if the tide had gone out and never returned. The hills have been rounded into soft feminine curves by the wind and sun, but between Copiapó and Arica, a stretch of nearly a thousand kilometres, there is only one river, the Loa, that flows throughout the year, carrying meltwater from the distant snows, and this has cut itself so deep into the plateau as to be scarcely visible.

Before reaching the Loa we crossed the 'Despoblado de Atacama', the empty land. It is a super-desert: the sun burns with an intensity reached nowhere else on earth. It is the driest place on the planet, and with one exception which later we were to film, it is completely without life. It has always been a desert since the land rose from the sea. At sunset the temperature can plunge from 40°C to zero in an hour, and sometimes the mountains echo with the unearthly thunder of rock splitting from the stress of the change in temperature.

One can stretch a sleeping bag on the sand and lie with an incomparable view of the Milky Way, and shooting stars, confident in the knowledge that there will not be a trace of dew, and not an animal for hundreds of square miles, and meditate on the unbelievable fact that the teeming jungle is the other side of the peaks where the moon rises as clear as if one were in space.

The coastal desert north of the Loa river is curious not only for its long thin shape, but for its high humidity and low temperatures. The sun is frequently obscured by mist, and it is about ten degrees Celsius cooler than the equivalent latitude on the Atlantic coast. This is the effect of the cold Humboldt Current which sweeps north along the coast of Chile and Peru from the wild southern latitudes of the West Wind Drift. At night a land breeze blows onto the cold sea and fogs condense, to be blown ashore by the sea breeze during the day. The sea breezes never bring rain because they are so cooled by the ocean that they have to rise thousands of feet before they are cold enough to drop their moisture. Yet in Lima a thick mist called the *garua* obscures the sun from June to December and droplets will wet the windscreen of a car, though the roofs of many buildings are made of mud which would melt if it rained. The rains in the mountains occur during the *Invierno Boliviano* (Bolivian winter) from January to March, so the few rivers that reach the coast are in spate when the weather is at its driest.

Along the edge of this empty coast cluster ports built to export the mineral produce of the interior. They are as dependent on outside supplies as ships on the ocean, and are a startling reminder of the artificiality of modern city life. Each is supplied with its life-lines from the mountains: water, electricity, and the highway. Walk down the main street festooned with all the usual plastic signs for whisky and Japanese electronics and you could be anywhere. But every stick of wood or sheet of metal comes by sea or over the desert. After the searing browns of the desert the flowers look brighter and the greens more green, but many of the towns are dying, life is expensive to maintain, and there is a sense of oppression, as if the sands of the desert are waiting.

In the interior, lost in a landscape as featureless as the sea, lie the skeletons of other towns: *oficinas*, relics of the nitrate boom, which at its height in 1912 employed 45,000 workers in 170 mines. There are still whole towns of barred shadows and creaking shutters lying empty to the desert wind, complete with their railway engines and bandstands and bakeries. Bread and circuses. In one I found an old horse-drawn hearse with its dusty black curtains still stirring, a reminder of the appalling human cost of dragging wealth from this wasteland. The cemeteries with their iron crosses are already half covered with sand drifts, and the bones of the mules that died carrying the nitrate to Antofagasta, which once were strewn all over the desert, have crumbled and been covered. Once Chilean Nitrate was the hottest property on the London stock-exchange. British capital owned it, British engineers built the railways that served it, British engineers staffed it. A British clock still repeats the chimes of Big Ben in Antofagasta but the mineral over whose deposits Chile, Bolivia, and Peru fought the War of the Pacific only one hundred years ago is forgotten and the British are gone.

The dryness of the Atacama Desert means that naturally occurring minerals have never been leached out by rain, and the cause of all this activity in such an unlikely and uninviting spot was caliche, the only commercially viable deposits of sodium nitrate in the world. The ore contained up to eighty percent nitrate at first, and was picked out by hand for making gunpowder. Later it was used for making nitric acid and as a high grade fertiliser.

The ore was concentrated in an area twenty to eighty kilometres wide and

700 long at a height of between 1000 and 2000 metres above sea level, around the edges of what was clearly a lake or inland arm of the sea before it was raised by tectonic movements of the earth's crust. The caliche lay beneath a few centimetres of overburden in a layer up to five metres thick. How it got there is still the subject of controversy, but most of the salts are very soluble and it is certain that they would never have remained there had they not been in the desert.

One theory is that their origin is volcanic, generated by acids from the magma. Another is that immense deposits of guano, the droppings of seabirds, once covered the shores of large salt lagoons and that these decomposed to form nitrate. Guano has indeed been found in small quantities within the nitrate fields, but there is a serious objection in that there is no calcium phosphate present there. This insoluble constituent of guano is unlikely to have vanished if the soluble sodium nitrate remained. Another hypothesis is that the nitrates came from the decay of great masses of seaweed growing in tidal lagoons. Small pieces of seaweed are still found within the caliche, and the presence of large quantities of iodine supports this explanation. Chile still produces two-thirds of the world's iodine from this area. Most of the small inefficient oficinas went out of business following the discovery in Germany, when that country was cut off from Chilean nitrate during the First World War, of a method of synthesising ammonia. But now with the price of petroleum ever-increasing, the remaining plants in the desert are obtaining a new lease of life.

There are still fabulous mineral prizes to be won in the desert. Only three years ago the St. Jo. company began exploration in the Andes of the Elqui valley only a few hours north of Santiago. They knew there was mineral there at a place called El Indio but they didn't know what. They found gold ore which is said to be yielding 8 kilos of gold a tonne, one of the richest strikes ever made. It is said that they recovered enough gold merely making the road and digging the abutments for the bridges to finance the whole development of the mine. The lorries that carry the ore have a machine-gun escort, and are followed by a pick-up so that if a rock falls off the back they stop and pick it up. It is now thought to be the richest single gold mine in the world.

The loneliness of the prospector crossing this most barren desert in the world would sometimes be disturbed at night in a most spectral way. In some areas far inland wings would beat the air and strange laughing cries would be heard, particularly when the mist called the *camanchaca* covered the land. In 1936 R.C. Murphy wrote in his classic book *Oceanic Birds of South America*, 'Sea fowl of sorts not yet properly identified still make their home in the dry valleys and gulches leading towards the nitrate pampas. An old resident [spoke] of a kind of "gull" locally called "garuma", which nests in such situations. The adults return only at night, bringing fish, and their cries are heard all through the hours of darkness. Such birds are unquestionably petrels.' Murphy did not know that garuma is the local name for the grey gull, the commonest resident gull on the Pacific coast from north Peru to central Chile. Nor did he know that

A.W. Johnson, who later wrote *The Birds of Chile*, had become so fascinated by the fact that he could find no nests of this species on the coast that he had tracked down a nesting colony in the desert in 1919. It was thus established that the grey gull is the only bird that is found on the sea coast every day of the year, yet never nests there.

Most of the studies since done on this bird, which nests in such an extraordinarily un-gull-like environment, had been made at a large colony east of Cerro Colupo near Pedro de Valdivia, about twenty miles inland from the nitrate port of Tocopilla. In 1942 30,000 eggs were taken away by lorry to be sold in Tocopilla, so it must have been a very large colony, but such depredations took their toll, and the colony is now deserted.

I very much wanted to film this gull that somehow hatches its eggs and rears its young in a desert where the surface temperature reaches 50°C. But despite the hundreds of thousands of gulls which feed along the desert coast, picking burrowing crabs out of the sand in front of the retreating waves, there was not a single known nesting colony in October 1980 when I arrived in Antofagasta. Thanks to John Fleming who was working for the local television station, and who had helped the BBC *Voyage of Charles Darwin* film crew, I was introduced to Prof. Carlos Guerra of the department of Oceanology of the University of Chile. He had a project on the grey gull, and in the hope of locating breeding grounds, had put advertisements in the local paper. He had had one letter saying that in 1930 the writer had worked at an *oficina* near Palestina where the railway from the south to Iquique crosses the line from Buenos Aires in Argentina to Antogagasta. There he had often heard the garuma and found nests. It seemed an incredibly long shot to follow up a report fifty years old, and looking at the map I saw that Palestina was over fifty miles inland. It was scarcely possible that gulls would fly so far from the coast every night, yet Johnson had written that nests had been found sixty miles inland at Aguas Blancas. I impressed on Prof. Guerra the need to look in other areas as well, and having discovered the tiny budget he had to work on, I gave him money towards petrol for his Toyota.

In January I was back with a film crew. Carlos Guerra had found signs of a colony, including an egg, after three nights spent searching an area on the side of Cerro Palestina. We spent the morning filming the grey gull feeding and flying and even mating on the coast, and then headed up the steep hill behind Antofagasta into the desert. At first we followed the main highway beside the railway towards Calama but then we turned off to follow the line to Buenos Aires past the O'Higgins station. 'Station' gives rather a grand interpretation to the wooden hut and carefully tended patch of green of this bleak outpost. From there the dirt track was grandly labelled as the B475 on my half-million scale map, but in practice it was a scarcely discernible scrape in the desert, crossed by innumerable unmarked trails. Drive across this desert and the tracks will be as clear twenty years later as they were the day after, so the area is a museum not just of Man's activities, but of his movements; and very confusing it is too. Carlos took us through an unmarked tank-firing range, spattered with shell holes, which fortunately was not in use that day, and on across the Salar de Navidad. There was a strong westerly wind blowing and as we ground in low gear over the bumpy surface we were enveloped in a stifling cloud of our own dust. The salar (salt flat) had a surface that looked exactly as if it had been ploughed, full of white protrusions. Carlos explained that the salts in the ground absorbed the water from the mists and grew upwards, producing the rough surface on their own. After two hours driving across the glare of the empty desert we rejoined the railway again at an abandoned station once used as the base for a maintenance gang. A water tank, two buildings and a sign saying Llanos (flats). Inside we found two railway employees installing a portable telephone for our use in case of emergencies – something that I had arranged that morning in Antofagasta. They had come up by rail-car. My crew were impressed. We were instructed how to signal a complex code of morse dots and dashes to get O'Higgins, and then we pressed on to Palestina twenty kilometres further up the line. Parked there was a splendid derelict 1900's railway carriage, complete with vestibules at either end, which we adopted as our base and a protection from the searing wind.

The 'promised land' was a broad shallow valley about fifty miles long, flanked by ranges of gentle peaks smoothed by the slow abrasion of the wind. The valley floor was swept clean of dust by the same wind which springs up sharply from seawards in the early afternoon, and it was overlain by a countless multitude of angular grey-brown stones of sedimentary and basaltic rock. These are lightly cemented in place, perhaps by the action of the sun, which over millenia has toasted the exposed surface to a darker colour than the underlying sand. It is almost exactly on the Tropic of Capricorn, 1600 feet above sea level. Beside our wagon was the small steel parallelogram where the two narrow-gauge tracks crossed, dividing Chile into four.

While Donaldo set up camp Carlos and I drove off across the desert towards the mountain Cerro Palestina. The surface was fairly hard but we had to keep going on some soft patches and had to keep a good look-out for gulleys where sometimes in the last few thousand years freak rains had cut meandering steep-sided channels. We found Carlos' original tracks and followed them, and then he took a bearing and we walked for half a mile. By a cairn he showed me a pale mottled egg. I was sure it must be addled. Nothing could survive unshaded in that heat. I picked it up and shook it – it was addled. There was not a sign of a gull, we had come all the way from Santiago and this was all we had to film – one addled egg. Would we ever find any more in the couple of days we had before we must move on? Then, as I moved to put it back in the bare scrape of a nest, a large chick ran away from us. I was absolutely amazed. There was no sign of an adult bird; nothing but the wind, the stones, and the setting sun. We retreated hurriedly. I did not want to reduce further what seemed to be a very slim chance of survival for that chick.

At 10.30 that night we returned along the track, and when we could drive no further we left the side-lights on to act as a beacon, and split up into pairs to make a radial search. It was a moonless night, but the light of the stars was enough to show us where to tread. It was a strange experience to walk across

Llaima volcano smokes above a forest of araucaria pine: monkey-puzzle trees

PREVIOUS PAGE   Osorno volcano and the river Petrohué

Aconcagua, the highest mountain in the Americas, 23,034 feet

Llamas and alpacas at 16,000 feet on the Chilean Puna with volcanoes Pomerape (left) and Parinacota (20,800 feet)

OVERLEAF   Guano birds, guanay cormorants and brown pelicans, Punta San Juan, Peru

Lomas fog-forest, tara trees and wind-eroded rock, Lachay, Peru

that emptiness. The wind had dropped and the silence rang in our ears. When Carlos and I had walked a couple of kilometres we began to hear the eerie laughing calls of gulls flying in from the coast to change over their guard on the nests – they never fly over the desert by day. We could hear the wing-beats and see black shapes blotting out the stars, but it was too dark to see the gulls except by the light of our torches. Then we began to hear the peeping of chicks in several widely-spaced areas a hundred yards away or more. We found a place where two smaller chicks suddenly ran away from us and three adults swung over our heads scolding with a three-note alarm call. I took a bearing on the lights of our van three kilometres away and we built a cairn.

Keenan did better. They were going back to their pick-up, having found nothing, when a gull got up and began to mob them. Martin Saunders the cameraman with us had the experience to look in the opposite direction to the one from which the gull first attacked. Nearby, only a few feet from the pick-up, Keenan shone his torch on two fluffy chicks too small to leave the nest.

I went back with Martin the next morning before sunrise and we backed up our vehicle to use as a hide. The sun rose a bright yellow in a clear blue sky. There was no moisture in the air to give it colour. The silence was not to be broken even by the rustle of a lizard or the tiny scratch of an insect's leg. A silence so total and an emptiness so complete that some people find it terrifying. A silence that is only broken on Fridays, when the train from Buenos Aires rumbles laboriously over the last ridges of the Andes before it quickens its descent to the Pacific at Antofagasta. It was wierd to scan this eye-aching emptiness and have one's gaze alight on a gull standing over a bare scrape, protecting two chicks from the sun with fluffed out feathers and drooped wings.

The nests were roughly 500 hundred metres apart, and the adults with their white heads and grey plumage blended so well with the desert that they were very hard to see even when we knew where they were. The nests would be impossible to find except by night, when they are revealed by the calling of the birds which remained silent during the day. The colony at Cerro Colupo had had nests on average only five to ten metres apart. If ours could be called a colony, it was only inasmuch as the adults could hear each other calling at night. There was no visual contact during the day – the ground was too uneven. If other colonies are so widely dispersed it explains why they have not been found. The gulls have good night vision, but to find an isolated nest in this featureless waste on a cloudy night sixty kilometres from the coast is quite a test of navigation. Undoubtedly this is the reason for the calling as the gulls fly home at night. They call and are answered by their mates on the nest.

I watched the gull as she stood over her chicks. Dust-devils were the only movement in the whole vast spread of the valley whose walls vibrated in a heat haze. One chick stood with its head between the female's body and the elbow of her wing, as if she was tenderly protecting it. It yawned and blinked at us. She would be there all day as the sun climbed to the zenith and sank again. She would turn to meet the twenty-knot wind from the west-south-west as it began suddenly in the afternoon, bringing relief from the 50°C heat. Not until ten at night would her mate arrive with food for the chick, and before dawn she would leave for a day by the sea.

Clearly it is an advantage for the gulls to nest in an area where there are no predators, but why should they have developed this extraordinary nocturnal migration over such a large distance? The clue may be those deposits of guano – and occasional mummified seabirds – found in association with the nitrate deposits. It may be that the grey gull used to nest beside the shores of the weed-filled sea lagoons where the nitrate formed, before the lagoons were lifted high into the Andes. The gulls carried on nesting in the same place; it was the sea that moved.

The junction between the Atacama Desert shore and the Pacific Ocean must be the most dramatic zoological contrast that our planet can offer. Within a few metres the almost totally lifeless sand is replaced by the richest waters in the world, where at times the fish can be seen packed as close together as sardines in a tin, except that all their heads point in the same direction.

But there are a few creatures that take advantage of this contrast, like the grey gull. Along the rocky shores a species of tropidurus lizard basks in the sun, and then when the tide goes down it creeps to the edge of the water. When a wave recedes it dashes onto the green weed of the half-tide rocks and grabs a mouthful. If this is successful it then goes further, hunting for small crustaceans amongst the weed. As the next wave foams in over the rocks it dashes away with its tail lifted in the air like the drawings of a dinosaur. It is a perilous way of earning a living, and it is very comic to watch.

One day I was sitting in a seaside fish restaurant having lunch with the film crew when I saw another unexpected example of this kind of opportunism. An oasis humming-bird (*Rhodopis vesper*) was hunting along the sea-weed on the edge of a rock-pool, picking out what I assumed to be marine invertebrates from the seaweed. There are two rivers which reach the coast at Arica and humming-birds are common, but I had never previously heard of one 'fishing'.

Even within the tropics of Chile and Peru, the sea is surprisingly cold, as anyone who has swum there will tell you. The Humboldt current sweeps up the entire west coast of the continent of South America as far as Cabo Blanco, just short of the Ecuadorian frontier, where the coast suddenly turns northeast towards the gulf of Guayaquil. This cooling is not only due to the speed of the current's flow, five to ten kilometres per hour, but also to the upwelling of very cold waters from the immensely deep Chile–Peru trench. The temperature of the water off Callao, the port for Lima Peru, is actually 3°C cooler than that off Antofagasta, Chile, over 1500 miles further south. Although the current is only about 100 miles wide it has a dramatic effect on the climate of the land. Along an immense distance of shoreline the climatic and physical conditions of the shore remain unchanged. It is as if from Norway to Gibraltar the climate and fauna were constant – there is no other coast like it in the world. The upwelling waters are also extremely rich in salts and micro-organisms which form the base of the food-chain responsible for the famous flocks of guano birds, and which for a short time made Peru the greatest fishing nation in the world.

The waters abounding in fish, and the stable climatic conditions, had another important effect. It is now believed that man's first steps towards an organised civilisation in South America, which culminated in the impressive engineering feats of the Incas, began on the coast. Traditionally it had always been thought that the growth of a sedentary civilisation, as opposed to a wandering hunter-gatherer way of life, the sort still practised until recently in Tierra del Fuego, depended on the cultivation of crops. But on the Peruvian coast the resources of the sea were so vast, and so easily harvested, that cities could spring up on the basis of fish alone.

It is not surprising that seabirds are frequent motifs in the decorations of the adobe walls of the early coastal cities, and are found in the designs of textiles and pottery over two thousand years old. They are by far the most spectacular feature of this impressive but monotonous coast. There are three main varieties: the guanay cormorant, which has been called the 'billion dollar bird' because of the value of its droppings or guano (Quechua for excrement), and is certainly the most valuable bird in the world from the commercial point of view; the Peruvian booby (a gannet) which has been much reduced in numbers by human disturbance; and the brown pelican, the ancient and improbable bird which has now overtaken the booby as the second most important producer of guano.

The guanay feeds solely on a fish called the anchoveta (*Cetengraulis mysticetus*, a different fish from the anchovies which we are accustomed to eat on top of pizzas). This fish usually forms an important part of the total biomass in the Humboldt Current. It feeds off plankton which migrates to the surface by day and sinks again at night. As the shoals swim through an area rich in plankton there is a constant rotation, the individuals at the front returning to the rear so that the whole shoal has an equal chance to feed. When danger threatens from predatory fish such as tunny, the shoal bunches close together. The cormorants set out from their roosts throughout the day in long undulating streamers which disappear into the mists of the horizon. When they find a shoal they fish from the surface where the water boils with the fright of the fish below. Diving and swimming they quickly satiate themselves and then sit on the water in dense black rafts, resting and digesting, until the flight home.

The boobies are rather more dramatic. They too fly in long lines but they twist and dive vertically into the water from a height of about twenty metres, folding their wings in the last split second, as they disappear in a fine splash of spray. The effect of a large flock suddenly diving is that of a waterfall as a seemingly unending supply of birds bombards the surface and hundreds flap off again to rejoin the diving mass. They too eat the anchoveta, and one of the most extraordinary sights this strange region can offer is when a large number of boobies flies over a shoal, and simultaneously, as if to a sergeant-major's command, all suddenly turn and plunge together so that a sky which was full of birds is left empty.

We filmed the boobies nesting on cliffs where they had built up plinths of guano on the edge of small ledges which were fluted by the droppings running down in a most decorative way, as if designed to show off the smart white and grey bird perched on top.

Pelicans are far more graceful in the air than they look on the ground. It is fascinating to watch them from the top of a cliff flying in lines, soaring in the rising air on the face of a breaking wave. When the wave begins to collapse the leader swings away to the wave behind and the whole file snakes after him. They fish by crash-diving at an angle into the water making a considerable splash, and enclosing a quantity of water inside the pouch of skin beneath the lower bill. As they lift their heads the water drains out and the fish remain. If they have the luck to hit a big shoal they simply scoop the fish up with their enormous bill, but they can never fish far below the surface.

It is an overwhelming experience to stand on the edge of a guanay colony in the early morning, when the air is filled with the sound of wings and drifting feathers. The birds on the ground move their long-necked bodies in waves like the wind blowing over a wheat-field. From prominences a constant stream of low-flying birds flaps towards the sea, wheeling downwind at the cliff-edge, their places filled from behind by a steadily marching mass of black-coated figures. Turkey vultures hang in the updraught from the cliffs, ever on the look-out for the casualties of so large a colony, and lizards dart about the desolate surface hunting for feather-lice. The cormorants scrape at the surface to form a nest, and build up rings of guano, like miniature craters with round rims, which are as close-packed as pecking-distance will allow: three nests to the square metre, housing six adults and six young. Such colonies are only possible where there is a huge food supply, and the build-up of ammonia from the droppings is so great that they can only exist where there are constant winds. Even the colour of the guano is important, as the greyish-white reflects the heat. The birds will not return to an old colony that has been cleaned off unless the rocks are painted white. From the shore, the islets off the coast look like miniature snow-capped mountains.

The value of the guano as a fertiliser was well known to the Indians before the Spaniards arrived, and they were good conservationists. The Incas forbade anybody to visit the colonies during the nesting season under pain of death. However, its value was slow to be realised by the Conquistadors. At the beginning of the eighteenth century guano was used in the irrigated valleys of north Chile and south Peru, exciting the wonder of travellers at the production of the land. A century later some forty boat-loads a year were being shipped from the Chincha islands in Peru up and down the west coast. The owner of a small brig could make a profit of $10,000 from a single trip. In 1840, twenty barrels arrived in England, where farmers were suspicious that the enormous crops resulting from its use would exhaust the soil. It was not long, however, before it was recognised that in terms of its nitrogen content it was more than thirty-three times as effective as ordinary farmyard manure.

An official Peruvian survey of 1847 claimed that there were more than twenty-three million tons of guano on islands off the coast, and that they would be enough to supply the world for 170 years. Ten years later sixty-two percent of the entire revenue of Peru was from the sale of guano. The best was the ancient guano which had accumulated to great depths over centuries. On the Chincha islands where 4.5 million birds nested, there were great domes of guano on top of the rock, which were up to fifty-five metres deep. These were quarried by slave labour and loaded into sailing ships for Europe and North America. In 1860, 433 vessels loaded at the Chinchas and all other known sources were being rapidly quarried, and by 1874 the deposits had been completely exhausted. The mining had been carried out on a year-round basis with no thought given to the survival of the birds. These were killed to feed the labourers, and hundreds of barrels of eggs were exported. It was not until 1909 that a national guano administration was set up to supervise a rational annual harvest, and one of their first actions was to prohibit access to the islands.

It might have been hoped that the Peruvians would have learned a lesson from history, but in the 1950s it began to be appreciated that whilst birds must digest twenty tons of anchovetas to produce one ton of guano, the same amount of fish could be processed to make four tons of fish-meal for use as a pig or poultry feed-supplement or even as fertiliser. Hundreds of small companies began to send out purse-seine boats to catch what seemed an inexhaustible supply of anchoveta; fish-meal factories sprang up all along the coast. At Chimbote alone there were more than thirty factories. Peru caught more tonnage of fish than any other country in the world in 1965 and the garua mist, which envelops the city of Lima, stank of fish-meal. It couldn't last. The population of anchoveta crashed, the plants went out of business and scores of new human settlements on the coast were left without employment. Twenty seven million dead and dying seabirds were washed up on the Pacific coasts. But they were not all simply victims of human greed. It is the nature of large dense populations of animals to be unstable, and despite the steady predictable pulse of the tides, the ocean currents are far less certain.

Every year in the summer the cold stream from the south encounters a southbound warmer current, which replaces or submerges the cold waters bathing the coast of northern Peru. As the summer progresses these warm, less saline, waters move further south before retreating again in the autumn. But on what is held to be a seven-year cycle, the atmospheric low pressure areas of the Pacific move further south. The warm current – called El Niño de Navidad (the Christmas Child) – rolls back the Humboldt current and flows southwards down the coast of Peru, sometimes reaching as far as Chile. The constant southerly winds give way to humid monsoon-like blasts from the north, the ocean temperature rises 8°C and the desert is flooded by torrential rain. It is a catastrophe not only for the teeming life of the Humboldt Current but for the coast, where agriculture and towns are quite unable to deal with the run-off from the rain. Rivers change their course, dry desert quebradas become raging torrents, irrigation channels are overwhelmed and mud houses collapse. The last major reversal of the current was in 1925 when almost two metres of rain fell on Lima instead of the normal five centimetres.

The effect of El Niño in 1965 was not so dramatic, but decimated the guano bird colonies. The cormorants flew south fruitlessly searching for anchoveta, and even left the sea to fly up river valleys to perch with the cattle egrets in the pastures in their desperate search for food. Whether the disaster was made worse by over-fishing, or even caused by it, or would have happened anyway, is impossible to say. But once again the Peruvian economy suffered a massive reverse.

The most attractive of the guano islands are the Ballestis group off Paracas. The islets are undermined by splendid caverns filled with clear turquoise water; groups of Humboldt penguins huddle in the depths and both the South American sealion and the South American fur seal come out to sport round visiting boats shouting their greeting with very human voices. By the sides of the cliffs, black-capped with birds, and sour with the smell of guano are the gantrys where the square-riggers used to rock their spars.

The fur seal (*Lobo fino*) was once hunted all over the southern oceans for its skin. One can gain some idea of the scale of the slaughter since between 1797 and 1804 fourteen American ships captured three million seals on the Juan Fernandez Islands off the Chilean coast. In 1883 a Chilean government survey found only two animals. Yet such is the power of recovery of the species that although Murphy could write in 1936 that the fur seal was 'a rare and almost exterminated mammal, at least within the Humboldt Current region,' we visited, at Punta San Juan, a guano colony on a point on the mainland, and found there eighteen thousand seals and sealions.

Although both species are protected in Chile and Peru they are still illicitly hunted all along the coast. In Tierra del Fuego they are used as bait. In north Chile Donaldo met a diver whose job was to hook a rope onto wounded seals that had slipped off the rocks after being shot. These were then taken to a sausage factory for human consumption. A Chilean whaling factory-ship, the *Juana*, is also operating in contravention of International Whaling Commission rules.

We watched the battle-scarred old sealion bulls sitting on top of their rocks defending their harems of females against young challengers, massive beasts with furry manes that really did make them look like lions. The sun sank behind them into the Pacific in a red incandescent disk crossed by lines of black guano birds, an unending stream in silhouette against the burning horizon.

We were there at sunset for a reason. To record one of the oddest relationships on this unusual coast.

Dr Aurelio Malaga Alba was a frail seventy-nine, but the twinkle in his eye had not dimmed. He had spent six years as a veterinary student in Edinburgh, and had three great passions: Christmas pudding, kippers, and vampire bats. We brought him a Christmas pudding from Bristol but the kippers had proved to be bad company in the desert. At the smart Las Dunas hotel in Ica he marched into the kitchen to instruct the staff how to prepare a mixed grill instead.

'Oh, and I'd like you to keep this in the fridge for me.' He took a large jar full of dark red fluid out of a paper bag.

'What is it?'

'Blood.' This was a huge joke, but they took the jar.

'And what's it for?'

'To feed the vampires, of course.' This doubled them up with laughter.

Meanwhile, thirteen vampires were hanging on the shower-rail of Dr Malaga's hotel bathroom. He would never keep his vampires caged at night, even if they had to fly loose in his own bedroom while he and his wife Mary slept under mosquito nets. Mary was amazingly tolerant of her husband's macabre enthusiasm. By the morning the bathroom would look as if it was the scene of a murder, with blood spattered all over the walls. She would have to clean it up before the hotel maid fainted on finding it.

Vampire bats are important to veterinary medicine because a small proportion of them carry rabies, which they transmit to cattle by biting them to drink their blood. Dr Malaga is a world expert, and had worked in Trinidad and Mexico, as well as throughout South America. Two of his assistants had died through contracting rabies from bites and while he was in Mexico between 1930 and 1960 there were 126 human deaths from vampire-bat rabies. For years he had kept a colony of bats for research at San Marcos University in Lima. Within three months of his leaving they were all dead from neglect.

Desmodus rotundus lives along the length of the Andes from Trinidad to Chiloé, feeding on animals to altitudes as high as 14,000 feet. It has long been known to the peasants who frequently fly a white flag over the corrals for their animals 'to keep off the vampires,' although they would not know a vampire if they saw one. The bats show a definite preference for biting certain animals. They are epicureans, according to Dr Malaga, and in descending order they prefer the blood of: donkey, mule, horse, cow, poultry, humans, and sheep. But vampires also live in the caves of the coastal desert, and as there is nothing else, they feed on the blood of sealions.

It is one thing to read that vampires have been known to feed on the blood of sealions, it is quite another to film it happening. That was where Dr Malaga and his bats in the bathroom came in.

Lucho Peña had known vampire caves and offered to take us to them. For three weeks he followed the desert coast of Chile for most of its length exploring every inlet. Everywhere the same story: plenty of people said there were vampire caves, but always they had been disturbed and the bats driven out or killed by the army of shell-fish gatherers who in the last twenty years had swarmed along the coast to raid the dwindling population of abalone and sea-urchins for the canneries. It could even be said that the vampire was becoming an endangered species. The only colony was miles from the nearest sealion.

In Peru the bats are more common, the coast is less accessible from the Pan-American Highway and fewer people can afford transport. Every day tourists who visit the famous Inca ruins of Pachacamac near Lima file unknowingly under an arch on which hang vampire bats. At Punta Juan there had been bat caves, but the caretaker for the guano corporation had cleared them out. As good conservationists we felt justified in reintroducing the bats there. At least that was our excuse.

It is probable that bats first got a taste for blood by eating insects that had fed on it, and they may have acquired the rabies virus at the same time. Most bat colonies have a very low level of latent infection, but when they migrate, or become crowded at breeding time, the stress reduces their resistance to the virus and it can build up to a lethal level. They then bite other animals to feed and an epidemic can begin. Dr Malaga pointed out that the latent infection was not only confined to bats. One unfortunate Frenchman was bitten by a dog known to be rabid but did not develop the disease. He thought he was safe, but a year later he had a violent argument with his mother-in-law; with the stress the virus emerged, and he died within ten days!

None of this could be described as good public relations for the vampire bat, and despite Dr Malaga's special pleading we viewed them with circumspection. One particularly fancied Martin's ankles and on one occasion he burst out of the door of the room in which they were confined and rushed down the corridor, pursued by the bat, hopping like a frog with wings. It went straight under the table, where we were in the middle of supper, scattering us in all directions and starting a wonderful chase, Dr Malaga shouting instructions.

During the summer when the sealions and fur seals give birth, condors fly down from the Andes to scavenge on the sudden wealth of placentas and dead animals in the ever-growing colonies. A famous place for this is Paracas, whose name means wind. One can stand on the desert cliffs with a superb view of rolling pinkish desert and the breakers foaming on the rocks offshore. Below, the sealions tumble in the waves and pelicans cruise over the wave-tops. The cormorants trail like whip-lashes across the sky and the condors soar past the edge of the cliff at eye-level only a few metres away. In winter the lagoons nearby are full of migrant waders and flamingoes. Every day a strong southerly wind blows up at noon, and the fishermen return to the snug cove behind the headland marked by an enormous candelabra-shaped carving hollowed in the cliff to seaward long before Pizarro landed on this coast.

At Sechura I drove into the desert to a camp where a group of scientists from Wisconsin had a project on condors. They had found fifteen nests but not one of them was in use. We scrambled up to one, climbing a quebrada baked dry by the sun but bearing all the evidence of torrential floods. A red-shouldered hawk was nesting on a promontory where it would catch the cooling wind. The mate arrived bringing food to the nest, a big, untidy pile of sticks, showing a lovely white underwing and smart black stripe on the white fan of the tail. We climbed down onto the condor's nest, a dusty grey ledge about six feet square, overhung by sloping rock. There was a rounded impression in the gravel and a few tiny scattered fragments of thick shell. The view was a wild one, of hills and glaring desert strewn with fossil sharks' teeth. It was bleak and impressive but very empty. The whole experience of the desert is of one vast void.

7

The Desert in Bloom
and the Life of the High Lagoons

One of the more disconcerting experiences that any minor exploration of the Peruvian desert is certain to bring, is to find oneself surrounded by human skulls grinning from the sand. Frequently they have crania deformed by being tightly wrapped when growing; frequently, too, they retain unpleasant quantities of mummified flesh and hair still adhering. These disturbing remains are a by-product of a major Peruvian illegal industry: grave-robbing. The ancient inhabitants of this coast well knew that the aridity of the desert would preserve the remains of their dead indefinitely. Modern Peruvians know that it also preserved their pottery, and especially their textiles. The textiles of Paracas are justly famous for their magnificent design and colouring, the fineness of the threads employed, and their preservation, although they are at least two thousand years old. It is a profitable trade to rob tombs and the practitioners are none too discriminating; some of the staring skulls wear collars and ties.

The aridity that preserves death is supremely hostile to life, yet where the Andean rivers managed to cross the desert to the sea many different ancient cultures sprang up, and not only became masters of irrigation, but also used another source of water: not from the land, but the air.

Travel up the Pan-American Highway in Peru is often made hazardous during May to November by the garua, the dense cold mist that rolls in condensed from the sea breeze by the cold Humboldt Current. This is worse during the night, but on steep west-facing slopes it can be dense during the whole day. It is a shock when travelling along a road that is only a notch cut in the side of a sliding sand-dune, hundreds of feet above a sheer unguarded drop to the sea, to look up in a patch of sunlight and see green trees on top of a mountain. These are the lomas, areas of woodland that drink fog.

In the whole of the month of August there are only thirty-six hours of sun in some lomas areas, and the average temperature is only 13°C, whilst at only 2600 feet, above the mists, the temperature rises sharply to 24°C. At one time, when the climate was not so dry, it is likely that these areas of woods and annual plants stretched in a fringe along most of this tropical coast, but with increasing aridity they became isolated pockets, ideal sites for different species to evolve. Now they have a very high proportion of endemic species (unique to the area). The vegetation itself draws moisture out of the air by condensation – a rain gauge under a tree measures up to eight times more precipitation than one in the open. Unfortunately this makes the lomas an extremely fragile ecosystem, and indiscriminate cutting of the trees for fuel, and over-grazing by goats, has reduced their area to a tiny fraction of what it was once. In pre-colonial times some lomas were terraced and used for growing crops. Others were the haunt of guanaco and puma.

One of the best known lomas just north of Lima is Lachay. The last white-tailed deer there – a fine male – was shot by the British Consul in 1931. In a desperate attempt to preserve the humidity, imported trees such as eucalyptus and casuarina were planted and fortunately beneath them there has been some recovery of the original flora. Lachay itself is now being rehabilitated with technical cooperation from New Zealand.

After the immense open space of the sunlit desert, Lachay is a strange secret garden. The mist blows in wraiths between the twisted branches of the tara trees, drops hang on the leaves. Granite boulders hunch against the side of the mountain, carved by wind and moisture into smooth hollows and black holes. The water condenses on the rocks, too, and runs down their sides – where succulents spring up to caress the lichen-covered surfaces with delicate tendrils which would not survive a day of fierce desert sun. Star-shaped leaves are beaded with hundreds of droplets as if after a heavy dew, and yellow calceolarias bob their heads when a breath of breeze stirs up the valley. The air has the dead claustrophobic feel of a damp cellar, and the half-seen outlines of a fox hunting through the green abundance, and a red-backed hawk circling in the mist, only add to the feeling that the place has an anima of its own.

A brilliant red jewel fluttered down from a tree to a tiny depression in the top of a rock: a vermilion flycatcher. Water had dripped until a bowl was hollowed, and had filled it. The bird took a bath in the middle of the desert. Over sixty species of flowering plants bloom in these rocky valleys, and reminded me of the delicate growth in spring beneath an English wood. Yet in summer they dry to a husk, and blow away in the wind, and it is as if they had never existed. The brown bare earth is reclaimed by the desert that lies all around.

The lomas are not the only phenomenon of the Atacama Desert that can delight the botanist and rest the eye from the glare of sun on rock. At the southern end, in the region of Copiapó in Chile, years totally without rainfall are frequent, and the countryside is bare rock, gravel, and sand, disturbed only by the dust-devils that twist and scurry across the valley floors. But once every five years or so, or sometimes after twelve, it rains two or three times in June, July, or August. I had written the result into my script, but I never thought it would happen.

Over the last five years the work of the Natural History Unit of the BBC has been affected hundreds of times by the weather failing to conform to the standard pattern, not just in the United Kingdom, but all over the globe. Usually it causes problems, but we seemed to be getting all the luck. At Cape Horn it was brilliant sunshine. Now Donaldo arrived in Arica, with his vehicle covered in mud, to report that the highway through the desert had been washed away by a downpour. Five months later, I spent a Sunday out at Lucho Peña's site near Santiago where he was building a remarkable ferro-concrete shell-roof laboratory to be used as a centre for his natural history foundation, and a base for visiting scientists. He assured me that in a few weeks time the desert would be in flower. It had last flowered in 1975 and I had seen the photos in Lucho's publication *Expedición a Chile*. I knew it was one of the wonders of the natural world.

I hired a helicopter because I wanted aerial tracking shots to show the scale of the phenomenon. It would also make it much easier to locate the flowers and then get to them by landing nearby – possibly far from the nearest track. This might save days of the cameraman's time and was a great advantage to set against the horrifying cost per hour of the chopper. Another stroke of luck was that only a week before it had snowed heavily, very late in the season. So I decided to fly north, cutting towards the mountains to take some aerial film of the foothills with Aconcagua behind.

Soon we reached a suitable craggy area and I asked the pilot to land so that we could take the door off for filming. I expected him to drop down into a valley below the snow line, but instead he did a couple of quick turns over a wind-swept ridge, where the snow had been blown clear, and then put us down at 8000 feet on a level icy patch no bigger than half a tennis court. While the mechanic took the door off, the cameraman and I unloaded every bit of weight we could: spare fuel, water (for the desert), tent, bolex, etc., to lighten the aircraft to improve our rate of ascent. Then we whirled off, leaving the mechanic standing alone on his mountain-top with our forlorn pile of equipment in a temperature of minus 5°C. I hoped we would be able to find him again.

I was a bit concerned about our flying at 12,500 feet with no oxygen, as we were not acclimatised, and with the door off it was exceedingly cold, but I explained the shot I wanted – skimming up the side of a cliff so that we got lots of movement in the foreground and then bursting over a ridge to reveal the marvellous panorama of Aconcagua beyond. I had not flown much in helicopters, and I found it difficult to get a point of reference to relate how high we were compared with what we were approaching. At full power we clattered up the icy precipice and skimmed over the snow and jagged rocks straight towards the ridge. For a stomach-tightening moment I thought we were going to hit it, but it flashed past a metre below the skids. Then the camera jammed because of the cold and we had to do it three more times! I found myself holding on very tight to the seat. Each time we shot over the narrow ridge it was like being catapulted over a precipice, and the ground fell a long long way below.

The flowers were supposed to begin at Vallenar, which takes its name from Ballenagh in Ireland, the birthplace of the O'Higgins family. Bernardo O'Higgins, the illegitimate son of a Viceroy of Peru, led Chile's revolt against Spain in 1810, and is the principal national hero. We swung towards the coast over the hills through which Darwin had ridden, writing that he was tired of using the epithets barren and sterile. But barren and sterile they were, and there was not a sign of any flowers.

The next day dawned cloudy so we could not film even if we found the flowers. We were in the middle of lunch when the cloud lifted and we rushed back to the airstrip. We flew north and after thirty miles we at last found a purple wash spread like a water-colour on the desert. We swooped in and landed in the middle of the thickest patch, cutting the engine. At once we were enveloped by a honeyed perfume that was almost overpowering. At my feet was pure sand, but all around us mauve flowers bobbed on their thin stems to the warm breeze. As far as we could see they spread over the undulating ground in a carpet of colour. Beyond, the mountains rose in the crisp dry ochre shades of the desert, and above, a blue sky was filled with scudding cumulus. None of us could speak, it was like a miracle. Had we not just flown for hour after hour across an unending lifeless expanse as dry as the moon? It was as if the stones themselves had burst into flower, and none of us was prepared for the staggering beauty of it.

The flowers here were known as the guanaco's paw(*Calandrina discolor*), of a genus with some sixty species in Chile. They grew straight out of the sand, and so close together that I could not help crushing them as I walked. They had thick fleshy leaves and the thinnest of stems. Mixed in with them were sheets of the pale lilac of the rather similar malvilla (*Cristaria*); both of them as simple as a poppy, and as beautiful. Here and there in startling contrast were a cluster of yellow trumpets of the añañuca (*Hippeastrum añañuca*), a lily that guards a bulb deep below the hot surface of the sand.

The beauty of this scene was all the more evocative because of its transience. In a few weeks the sun would have dried this wonderland to a crisp and the winds would scatter the dry husks until only the memory remained. Amidst this mauve sea our scarlet helicopter looked like a giant insect from another planet, and suddenly I realised that I had not seen a single bee. What could pollinate this mass of blooms?

As the afternoon lengthens the flowers close up, and as we flew, first towards the coast, and then back up the Huasco Valley, I searched in vain for other sites, because I hoped to find other shades of colour. I had a second look at one mountain called Cerro Tomate. Why would it be tomato mountain if it did not turn red? My hunch was right. In the morning we flew there and the faint bloom of green I had noticed was transformed; the flanks of the ridges facing north were awash with flowers.

Here the vegetation was much richer. We were in the coastal desert zone where two kinds of cactus sparsely covered the northern slopes. One was a dome-like cluster of squat growths: the copiapó, which gives its name to the nearby town. But the cacti were swamped in a purple sea of annuals, shiny wet-looking leaves of creeping vines, yellow and red añañucas, two kinds of narcissi, alstromerias. Even the cacti were in flower. It was like an immense garden.

Other than Lucho's friends we only knew of one couple who had gone to look at the flowering of the desert that year. In Santiago no one even knew it was happening.

If the Paine Mountains made me fall in love with the Andes, there was another place that had burned images deep in my mind: the harsh highland desert – the Puna – on the border of Chile with Argentina and Bolivia.

In the south, and at the Equator, the Andes are a fairly narrow range; impressive for their height and as a barrier determining the climate and the range of species, rather than for their area. But in the central third of the South American continent, from northern Chile to Southern Ecuador, the range has spread. Nowhere in the world, outside Tibet, is there so large an area at so high an altitude. The rainfall increases from south to north and this determines three zones: the Puna in the south and the wetter Paramo in the north, whilst in the centre, between the western and eastern ranges of the Andes is a complex of lower plateaus, the Altiplano. The average height of the Altiplano is between 12,250 and 14,000 feet. This large area of highlands has had a profound effect on the biology of the continent. But first, a little more geology.

A normal thickness for a continent forming part of the earth's crust is thirty to thirty-five kilometres. Beneath the central Andes it is an abnormal seventy kilometres – a measurement only equalled beneath the Himalayas. As the mountains rose they had to be supported by the crust floating deeper in the fluid mantle. Hence the extra thickness. The volcanic landscape that now dominates the Andes only began to emerge some fifteen million years ago. (*Australopithecus*, the ape-like forerunner of man, existed ten million years ago.) Most of the great ice-capped volcanoes, that can be seen from ships far out at sea as they line the crest of the Andes, belong to the last four million years, and the great thrust of magma rising to form them caused extensive folding and faulting in the Altiplano and eastern ranges to form narrow but high mountain chains, whilst sediments running down from both east and west filled the Altiplano basin to a depth believed to be about fifteen kilometres, with a great V shaped wedge, reaching further below sea level than the peaks are high. Activity appears to have quietened down, but there is some evidence of the crust stretching beneath the Altiplano, and Lake Titicaca is a long depression – a kind of rift valley on a minor scale – between fault lines.

From the first concept of the series I had always considered aerial filming to be indispensable to show the scale and grandeur of the Andes, particularly over the Puna. Once again the only suitable aircraft was a Twin Otter of the Chilean Airforce, which they generously agreed to fly up from Santiago.

I had had so many problems with planes in Peru and Ecuador that I was relieved to see it arrive at Calama, 750 miles north of Santiago, dead on time.

We took off the next day into a perfectly clear sky. Even the east wind, which we had been warned would cause turbulence, did not appear, and we flew smoothly round the massive burnt peaks of the twin volcanoes San Pedro (20,190 feet) and San Pablo. On the western summit of San Pedro yellow deposits of sulphur gleamed in the pearly light and wisps of blueish smoke warned of the sleeping violence below. (It erupted last in 1911.) The air was hazy, but we could still see across range upon range of volcanic peaks stretching along the axis of the Andes. There were giant volcanoes at every stage of creation and erosion. There were little cones a few metres high – no more than dumps of cinders. There were perfectly conical scoria cones only a hundred metres or so tall. They looked like toys, playthings of the god of fire, until one saw the ragged lava flows that spilled from them across the plain like milk froth boiled over from a saucepan – yet the colour of a dead coal fire. It could have happened yesterday, so clear were the outlines.

The base on which these cones stood was a gently sloping plain of ignimbrite which had lapped in a pinkish flood around the feet of some of the older cones, and on the bigger cones themselves it was easy to pick out the sagging lava flows, and areas where hot avalanches had cascaded burning down the slopes. It was all so well preserved by the dry climate that flows hundreds of years old looked new, and, without a blade of vegetation to cover them, the colours were startling.

All the more so, because between the mountains lay huge white expanses of salt and borax – salars – all that remains of deep lakes which once covered much of the area between the mountains over which we flew and the younger eastern chain of the Andes.

We were flying with the co-pilot's window open to film from, and the rear door removed so that I could take photos. I had to keep rushing from one end of the plane to the other, to shout instructions in Spanish to the pilot and then run back to my perch on the floor by the open door. We were flying at up to 20,000 feet so we had to breathe oxygen via plastic tubes and bags plugged into the side of the plane, so each time I moved I had to plug myself in again. I also had a rope tied round my waist to prevent me from falling out of the door and I got so excited by the view and the shots we were getting that I kept getting hopelessly tangled up.

Donaldo, who has an amazing lack of instinct for self-preservation had gone up wearing flip-flop sandals. It was −12°C outside and the door was open. I watched his feet slowly turn blue, but he assured me they didn't feel cold.

I had hoped to persuade the pilot to trespass across the frontier with Bolivia so that we could film the strange pink Laguna Colorada, only fifteen kilometres away, the home of the James's flamingo. But it was exactly the time when Chile and Argentina were due to reply to Pope John Paul in answer to his arbitration on their border dispute in the Beagle Channel. The dispute had very nearly flared into war two years earlier. If Argentina attacked Chile – which from their belligerent remarks and state of preparedness seemed quite possible – Bolivia and Peru were likely to attack Chile simultaneously from the north, to try to reclaim the territory over which we now flew, won by Chile a hundred years ago in the War of the Pacific.

The only reference to the delicacy of the international state of affairs was that the pilot politely asked us not to photograph any Chilean installations. But he dared not cross the Tocotocare range for fear of starting a war. I had also hoped to film the magnificent cone of Licancabur (19,425 feet) and its twin volcano, Juriques, from the Bolivian side (the frontier passes through the summits) to get the pea-green Laguna Verde in the foreground, but there were a number of Bolivian military vehicles in full view, on what looked like newly-graded roads. No doubt they were extremely suspicious of our flying up and down as we filmed repeated takes of the volcanoes, but it saddened me that this spectacular area, a natural no-man's land, should have been turned into a military playground.

At this point we started running out of oxygen, and all had to unplug our masks so that the pilot had what was left. We didn't argue! We finished our filming at a more comfortable altitude, and got back to Calama with a little fuel to spare. All of us were dazed by the repeated decompression and recompression as we went up and down from 12,000 to 20,000 feet, and I for one was glad to have my feet back on the ground.

After a celebratory lunch with the aircrew, we drove the rest of the day south-west across the desert to El Tatio to film the highest geyser field in the world. The road was good but steep, and the combination of rarefied air and heavy loads meant that we only just had the power to get up the gradients by taking a run at them. We camped in the comfortable headquarters of a scheme which once was going to develop the thermal energy of the area for electricity. I insisted that everybody had only a light meal, but even so we slept badly, and after a night of pounding hearts, the next morning several of us had splitting headaches, one of the symptoms of altitude sickness or soroche. We were at 14,500 feet.

At sunrise huge pillars of steam rose from the floor of the valley and bubbling pools of water, boiling at only 86°C., had built little cones and chimneys of crystallised silica and chlorides. Where the water spilt over onto the ground it cooled and was invaded by heat-resistant algae which stained the runnels with the riot of colour of an Expressionist painting.

At midday we returned to the tiny sun-beaten colonial town of San Pedro de Atacama, at half the altitude, and headed off along the road towards Argentina.

We ground slowly up the Puna again, the sloping layer of ignimbrite cut by vertical-sided gorges filled here and there with patches of green growth. Volcanoes towered above us and it was extremely hot and dry. The glare was intense. As we went higher, the vegetation appeared from the desert – sparse tussock-grass and cactus. We saw a group of Darwin's rheas the high-altitude race of the bird we had met in the Paine Mountains, and once passed three male vicuñas, the delicate deer-like relative of the guanaco, so busy with their family squabbles that they didn't see us until we were close, when they galloped off, their golden fleeces and the white dust-spurts from their hooves back-lit by the low sun. The grass was brilliant yellow and the lava-flows jet black. The landscape was so theatrical that it was like driving through somebody else's dream.

We chugged over a slow pass at 14,300 feet, skirted a massive lava flow, and before us was our destination – Laguna Lejía. Lucho Peña had assured me that horned coots nested in the lagoon. Horned coots are confined to a few high lakes in the Andes of Chile, Bolivia and Argentina and are a puzzle because they have a curious fleshy proboscis that hangs like a black wattle over their bills. Nobody knows what it is for.

The light was now low, we were surrounded by splendid volcanoes, and the blue lagoon was crowded with flamingoes. But while we filmed I became more and more certain that nothing was nesting on the lagoon. Coots make nests of water-weeds and there was no sign of any plant life in the water. There was a bitterly cold west wind blowing, rolling balls of white salt froth from the wavelets of the lagoon across the desert. The light would soon fail, and the temperature would drop fast to well below zero. We were short of fuel, and feeling very tired from the glare and the altitude. I began to rack my memory about other possible nesting sites.

We drove on another ten kilometres to Aguas Calientes, a salar with small lagoons, hoping to see signs of coots. Instead I noticed a faded sign stencilled on a rusty lid of an oil can. With some difficulty we made out the word *Minas*. We were in the middle of a mine-field.

Retracing our tracks with care, we returned to pitch our tents by the bleak but safe shores of the Laguna de Lejia, where at least we should have a splendid view at dawn. I had hoped for a spectacular sunrise over the volcanoes, but the sun came up as a clear yellow ball in a blue sky, at once bringing a little warmth to our ice-covered tents. There was not a breath of wind, and the flamingoes were standing over their pink reflections so that it made their legs seem twice as long as normal. The silence was broken only by the cry of Andean gulls and the gabble of Andean geese, the biggest of the South American sheld-geese. I walked a few kilometres along the eastern shore of the lagoon with my binoculars. If there were gulls, there might be other bird-life. A spit of salt had separated a thin crescent of fresh-water lagoon from the bulk of the salt-water. It was covered in a thin layer of ice, and big fluffy gull chicks were sliding about on it trying to keep their balance. There was a thin fuzz of vegetation along the shore, and suddenly I noticed a coot's nest, a highly conspicuous pile of waterplants in full view of the shore. A solitary horned-coot's nest: Lucho had been right after all.

We filmed the two adults feeding their fluffy black chicks on the edge of the salt spit, with a volcano behind. They pulled fragments of weed from the water's edge and handed them to the chicks. Their 'horns', black and tasselled, simply drooped over their bills. The horned coot is officially a very rare bird that nests only over a height of 10,000 feet in a restricted area. But I find it a little difficult to get excited about a rare creature, if, when you get to its habitat, it is one of the most conspicuous animals present. Far from being the dramatic unicorn-like animal its name suggests, the horned coot was basically another boring black bird. Why then had we come to film it?

In 1946 W.R. Millie, a Chilean rancher and naturalist, examined some nests with the aid of a rubber boat and reported that they were built on top of conical mounds of stones 'built up from the bottom of the lake to a height of about two

The Chilean desert in flower

PREVIOUS PAGE   Añañuca lily and calandrina flowers in the desert

OPPOSITE ABOVE   Narcissi and OPPOSITE BELOW
Alstromerias flowering in the Atacama desert

ABOVE   Lomas fog-vegetation at Lachay
RIGHT   Calceolaria

50

OPPOSITE ABOVE   South American sea-lions
BELOW LEFT   Humboldt penguins
BELOW RIGHT   Guanay cormorants

ABOVE   South American sea-lions and fur-seals

OVERLEAF   Guano birds in sunset, and sunrise over geysers at El Tatio

53

ABOVE
Geysers at El Tatio

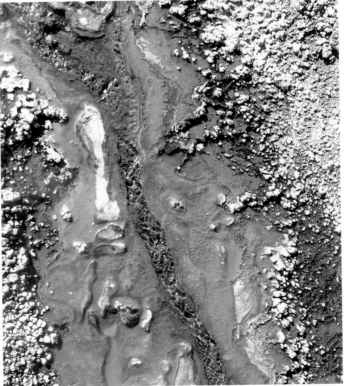

Algae colour a hot
spring

54

ABOVE
Mountain viscachas

RIGHT   Horned coots

ABOVE   Los Patos pass, Puna, Chile

OPPOSITE ABOVE   Volcano San Pedro
BELOW   Volcano Licancabur and Laguna Verde

LEFT Puna near El Tatio
BELOW Vicuñas

OPPOSITE Volcano
Aguas Calientes and
Andean flamingos,
Laguna de Lejia

Andean hillstar
humming-birds sip some
of the 20,000 flowers

63

64

feet and with an area at the top of approximately 10 square feet. The stones for the cone foundations were picked up one by one from the lake shore or from the bottom in shallow water and carried in the bill to the nesting site with both members of a pair taking part in this arduous task.' A most remarkable activity for a bird. He also reported that the coots used their 'horn' to convey water weed to build up the nests.

Coots usually build nests from aquatic plants, and nobody other than Millie has ever seen the coots build stone piles. They can certainly nest without them, but then the coots have hardly been studied at all. Our nest did not have any stones within a hundred and fifty yards or more. As for the horn, it certainly was not being employed to gather weed to feed the chicks in January. Possibly during the mating season in November, when it may be erected as part of the courtship display (other coots use their coloured frontal shields) it may get accidentally tangled up in the nesting material which is dragged in quite bulky bundles onto the nest. The giant coot, which occupies a very similar habitat, drags vegetation to the nest in exactly the same manner without the aid of a proboscis.

Anyone who will brave the lightning and ice of the '*invierno Boliviano*' and camp for a few weeks in the cold can find out. But the words 'horned coot building stone platform' had to be dropped from my script.

8

Life on the High Plateau: the Puna and the Altiplano

In the southern hemisphere summer begins in December, winter in June, and spring in September. In the high dry plateau of the Puna, nearly three quarters of the annual rain falls in January and February, and because of the cold it falls mostly as hail, sleet, and snow. As the rest of the year is dry and sunny, it is also the time of the year when the grass grows, and when most animals give birth.

Compared with a continental climate like that of the central U.S.A., the climate is not extreme, but it is a cold harsh land. The average temperature is only 2°C., and the daily variation is impressive – from minus 15°C. to plus 20°C. in the shade. The daytime temperatures in the tropical sun would be far higher but for the thin air and the lack of moisture in it. So greatly does the temperature depend on the sun, that a passing cloud can cause a temperature drop of 15°C. in five minutes. Another important factor is the westerly wind, which blows with considerable force during the afternoons and evenings making the cold far more acute.

The Puna begins in Chile at an altitude of about 12,000 feet, where the first growths of perennial bunch grasses and low evergreen shrubs appear. It ends where it is too cold for seeding plants to survive, at 16,000 feet – an altitude to which many of the glaciers of the bigger mountains descend, for even in the tropics there are many. So much of the rainfall is concentrated in the brief summer that for most of the year it is effectively a desert.

Another vital factor at these altitudes is the lack of oxygen, which is carried to the brain and muscles by the red blood corpuscles. Animals like the llama and vicuña have very high red corpuscle counts (the vicuña has fourteen million per cubic millimetre against Man's five to six million). This gives them far better adaptation to altitude. Man and other animals can adapt somewhat by increasing their population of red blood corpuscles and using an increased area of their lungs; but at high altitudes all animals from lower levels will hyperventilate – involuntary fast breathing – which expels carbon dioxide in large amounts, causing the blood to become alkaline. The amount of carbon dioxide or acidity of the blood is used in the body as a measure of the need for oxygen. (At sea level little carbon dioxide means plenty of oxygen.) So with hyperventilation the body is tricked into believing that there is plenty of oxygen and blood flow to the brain is reduced, starving, and eventually killing, brain cells. This is what causes altitude sickness, and what we had felt at El Tatio.

Curiously, birds do not appear to respond in the same way, and there are a number of birds that migrate over high mountains. Others have adapted both to high altitudes and to sea level where the climate is similar. So the rhea, the Chilean flamingo, buff-necked ibis etc. are found on the Puna and in Patagonia. Another curious fact is that although the air is so much less dense, birds do not appear to have any problem in flying, although the airport for La Paz, the capital of Bolivia, at 13,300 feet needs an immensely long runway for jets to gain enough speed to get airborne. There are flightless birds in the Andes – a grebe on Lake Titicaca, for example – but this is probably owing to a lack of predators rather than the need for too much effort.

In a landscape devoid of trees, birds nest on the ground, or in crevices or burrows where they are insulated from the extreme temperatures. Even a woodpecker – the Andean flicker – digs a burrow, often in a cliff overlooking a stream or the cutting of a road. This is the bird that is responsible for the Indian legends that it carries a special plant in its beak to dissolve the rock to make a hole. The truth is far more prosaic in that it is seen carrying nesting-material into an already existing hole! Many plants at high altitude grow in a cushion form to conserve heat and moisture, and I watched an Andean flicker hammering away at the edge of the nearest thing to a tree in those open grasslands, the yareta, a bright green bubble-like growth reminiscent of brain coral. It is sticky and almost rock-like to the touch, but it is composed of thousands of rosettes of tiny leaves. These strange green cushions grow up to a metre high and can cover as many as thirty square metres. Such growths are extremely ancient, several thousand years old, for the plant grows only 1.5 millimetres a year. Sadly, these strange plants make a good hot fuel and they are disappearing far faster than they are replaced.

The Lauca park in the extreme north of the long thin ribbon of Chile is a monument to the way Nature can heal herself if given the opportunity. When the park was declared in 1970 it was thought that there might be only five hundred vicuña left in the whole of Chile, so much had they been hunted for their pelts and wool – the finest in the world. But by 1980 there were over 7500 in the Lauca park alone. Not only have the vicuñas recovered, but once hunting was stopped the whole eco-system rebounded. The Lauca park is home for several interesting high-altitude species, most of which live around the areas of permanent water, the cushion bogs called *bofedales*, at a height of about 14,000 feet. In the early morning, the hummocky vegetation through which the water trickles, is covered in ice flowers, and even in the middle of the day the clumps are frozen solid inside. In the evenings, in the low yellow light, these frozen green hummocks become the playgrounds of a delightful little mouse with huge round ears, *Auliscomys boliviensis*, just one of the very large number of small rodents that have developed in different habitats in the Andes.

Originally there would have been chinchillas in the park, but there are still plenty of a close relative of the chinchilla, the viscacha. They live throughout the Andes from Patagonia to central Peru, where they form colonies of up to eighty individuals. They are the size of rabbits, and look very much like them, except that they have long fluffy tails which they use like squirrels for warmth and balance. But despite the superficial resemblance they are not related to rabbits, and are rodents. We would watch them creep out of the chill depths of the tumbled rocks to sun themselves in the early morning, each to his favourite sheltered cranny which would be defended vigorously against intruders. If alarmed they would scatter with great agility, leaping from rock to rock to disappear in an instant, but here they were relatively tame, and we could watch them wiggling their long drooping black whiskers like sleepy mandarins. In the evenings they would graze with the mice on the cushion bogs, usually with one animal keeping watch, ready to alert the others with a high warbling whistle to the danger of a passing eagle or fox.

The fur of the viscacha does not last, but their flesh was prized by the Indians, who also learned to domesticate the guinea-pig for food. A family had to be well off to have enough llamas or alpacas to provide protein, and in most Indian huts the family bed is raised from the floor with a space for guinea-pigs underneath. It seems rather murderous to eat animals that have shared your home, but they make a delicious stew. We were able to film wild guinea-pigs on a wind-swept plateau, but they were extremely wary, waiting motionless for hours in the entrance to their burrows, watching for any unexplained movement that might indicate danger. Then they would scurry across the open with an extraordinary jerky motion as if they were clockwork toys in need of a drop of oil.

The Puna is a hard place for any cold-blooded animal, and indeed there are only two reptiles found there: a non-poisonous snake and an iguanid lizard, *Liolaemus*, which comes in such a variety of shapes and colours that its Latin name is *multiformis*. It can survive even at 16,000 feet because of special adaptations and habits that are really rather curious.

The lizards live in burrows beneath stones or the roots of tola bushes where the night temperature is probably about 4°C. Yet they can walk and turn over very slowly with a body temperature as low as $1\frac{1}{2}$°C., and within minutes of emerging into the sun they warm to 20°C. They manage this because their colour is darker when they are cold – to absorb more radiation, and because they at once seek an insulating base like a tuft of grass where they can tilt their body so that the sun falls squarely on to it. In this way they can achieve and maintain a body temperature that is startlingly higher than that of their surroundings. When the air temperature is 0°C. their bodies can be as warm as 31°C. The need for protection and adaptation was all too apparent when accidentally we left a lizard, which we had caught for filming, in a box in our vehicle overnight. The temperature fell to minus 17°C. that night, and the poor lizard was frozen as stiff as a board.

While we were filming in the Lauca park we stayed at the Indian village of Putre at 11,500 feet where it was warmer and easier to sleep as there was more oxygen. We were lucky to see a taruca, the northern form of the huemul which lives between 9000 and 13,000 feet as far north as Peru. It had come down to graze on the irrigated fields of alfalfa. The villages of the true highlands, like Parinacota at 14,400 feet, are associated in most people's minds with the llama and the alpaca. Perhaps the photograph that typifies the Andes more than any other is a group of these animals, decorated with the coloured tassels that the Indians thread in their ears at Carnival time, set against a volcano.

Llamas and alpacas are now wholly domestic animals, but are probably descended from similar wild forebears. The llama is the bigger of the two, recognisable for a squarer outline and a tail that sticks out away from its body. Both of them are found in colours shading from black to white, and indeed they are often piebald with many mixtures of colours. Alpacas are used principally for their wool and meat, since they are more temperamental than llamas which are the traditional beasts of burden of the Andes, carrying up to fifty kilos for long distances. It is an odd sight to see a group of pack-llamas waiting to be loaded, a ring of woollen rope encircling their necks, resting on their backs, which they will not duck underneath to escape.

Both species are camelids, related to African camels, but more closely to the wild guanaco and vicuña. There is no doubt that they were extremely important to the pre-conquest civilisations of the continent. Without the discovery of the wheel, the only heavy transport was with teams of slaves or llamas, and they were used as much on the coast as in the mountains, where they were so sure-footed that many of the roads had flights of steps. Nowadays guanacos are seldom found over 11,500 feet, whilst llamas and alpacas will be seen up to 16,000, but this may simply be a reflection of the diminishing range of the guanaco.

Unfortunately the fertility of alpacas is low, especially when males and females are herded together, as is usually the case. This has led to the Indians abandoning them in favour of sheep and cattle on the better watered areas of the Altiplano. This in turn has serious ecological consequences, not only because of overgrazing, but because of the different feeding habits and the hard hooves of the imported species. Sheep require imported grasses which need fertilising, whilst alpacas and llamas survive on the native grasses which are far more resistant to erosion. Camelids have deeply-cleft feet, and walk on horny pads rather than hooves which cause less damage to fragile plants. Since their introduction in the sixteenth century, horses, sheep, and goats have caused untold destruction in the Andes. It is likely that most of the Altiplano was once covered by forests of polylepis trees, which are now confined to a few hollows and lower slopes. European man and his animals that browse on and trample young trees destroyed immense areas of this forest, just as the forest is destroyed in Patagonia today.

The fourth camelid, the vicuña, is the only ungulate which, like rodents, has lower incisors that grow continuously. This is probably so that it can cope with the hard bunch-grasses of the Puna, like the sharp-tipped festucas, which are hard enough to inflict painful wounds, but stand up above the snow. It is a creature of the Andean solitudes, never venturing below 12,000 feet, and there are few sights more beautiful than to watch a band of these graceful antelope-like animals walking past one of the great volcanic peaks in the incomparably clear light of an Andean morning.

Although usually mispronounced (with the Spanish ñ they should be called vicunia not vycuna) they have become famous for the soft fine wool that grows in a tuft like a bib below their necks. While the finest merino sheep wool measures thirty microns, vicuña measures ten. The Incas were well aware of the value of this wool, as they were of other fine animal products. (The Emperor Atahuallpa even had a coat made from the skins of vampire bats.) They managed the bands of vicuñas which were herded up once a year by encircling them with a large body of men, and driving them towards a funnel of stone walls. This *chacu* was until recently carried out at carnival time, and was followed by a presentation of animals or wool to the local dignitaries. Nowadays, in place of the taruca or vicuña, a fox or a lamb is presented as token game to the governor. The high Puna has been hunted bare.

The problem began because a vicuña yields only about half a kilo of wool a year (an alpaca may give seven kilos) and with the replacement first of totalitarian Inca rule, and later of the powerful landed aristocracy, by a freer society, the Indian discovered he could earn more simply by shooting vicuña for their skins. In the early 60's rugs were on sale in La Paz made from the foreheads of young vicuñas, and in Potosí a vicuña wool shawl cost only twenty dollars. Between 1954 and 1969 the population crashed by 96 percent. Local laws banning the killing and sale were ineffective then as they are now. (There is still a German-Chilean manufacturing vicuña cloth in Chile which is sold illegally by the better tailors of Santiago.) It was only after the signing of the Washington Convention on trade in endangered species by the USA and later by Britain, and the imposition of checks on the *import* of vicuña products into the wealthy developed countries, that the bottom fell out of the illegal trade. At the same time conservation pressure groups, particularly in Peru, had ensured that reserves were set aside and manned with guards, who on occasions had pitched battles with poachers.

The aim of the governments of Chile and Peru was to reestablish the vicuña as a productive resource, and later to harvest the wool in a rational manner. At Pampa Galeras, the principal reserve in Peru, there was by 1975 already an over-population in certain areas due to the successful recovery of the animals. The government claimed that between 1964 and 1979, 1000 animals had increased to 43,471. Within a few years the same will be true in the Lauca park. This is an inevitable consequence of Man conserving a wild population in a restricted area if there are no natural predators – in this case the puma. When those managing the Pampa Galeras park began to kill part of the excess male population there was an international outcry. Certainly they carried out the culling with little thought to public relations. I was in Lima at the time, and the first news Peruvians had of vicuñas being killed was on the radio; advertising vicuña meat on sale in the state-owned supermarkets. They also broke an international treaty with the other countries that are the home range of the vicuña, which prohibited any trade or killing without prior agreement between the signatories. The conservationists argued that the sale of any vicuña products gave carte blanche to poachers to move in, and they fiercely contested the population figures. The 'rational exploiters' argued that without management there would be serious overgrazing followed by starvation and epidemics – a situation exacerbated in the three years up to 1980 by a prolonged drought. They claimed that in 1979, ninety-one percent of the young died, and that since 1977 the population had been falling. This brought them into conflict with the 'conserve-at-all-costs' lobby, particularly from the USA. The ensuing battle of words became ever more political, not only within Peru, but between the developed countries of the northern hemisphere and the less developed of the south, an atmosphere in which it has been almost impossible to discover the truth.

Some family groups of vicuña have been successfully transferred to other parts of the Peruvian Andes, but this is extremely costly, and their protection in their new homes cannot be assured. Peru already spends more on Pampa Galeras than all its other national parks and reserves combined, and it can be argued that the fate of the animals within the huge Manu park which includes a whole range of habitats, from Puna to tropical lowland rain forest, is far more important than that of the vicuña.

One result of the high mortality of vicuñas at Pampa Galeras has been the appearance of large quantities of condors – up to sixty-five have been seen on a dead animal. This reminded me of Julio Prado's stories of condors attacking young animals. Carl Koford, who made a study of vicuñas, wrote that about half their young were either still-born or died shortly after birth, and that condors would attack them, the greatest danger being before the fawn had the strength to walk about, some thirty minutes after birth.

Besides providing some really startling scenic effects, the huge salars (salt flats) of the Puna usually have small lagoons round their edges which are the home of three kinds of flamingo. I had been told that there were many at the salar of Surire, which we reached after driving south across the desert on a bad track. We discovered that fifty soldiers were sleeping on the floor of the Surire police post, so we moved in with the hospitable watchman of some abandoned borax workings on the salar. It was so cold, even inside the hut, that I had to sleep with my hat on.

I got up at dawn to find that it was snowing. The eastern horizon was obscured, but there was a luminous glow brightening the showers of snow that were sweeping across the dark volcanic mountains to either side of the pure white salar. The sweeping clouds and the towering cumulus above them gave a scale to the scenery that was absent when it was clear. It was very grand and very lonely.

Flamingoes are extraordinarily highly specialised birds which developed about thirty million years ago. So they are twice as old as the Andes. Their ridiculously long legs enable them to wade out into deep lagoons or mud where they can feed in water ten times as salt as the sea. They feed by hanging their heads down between their legs until the front part of the bill is parallel with the ground – upside down. Their food consists of huge quantities of tiny organisms which they filter from the water by means of lamellae rather similar to those in the mouths of some whales. Flamingoes separate their food from the water by pumping water in through one side of the bill and out through the other, the food being caught on the fine mesh of the lamellae. This is achieved by moving the tongue in and out of the bill. As it is withdrawn it both creates suction and also scrapes the food organisms off the lamellae. The bill of the Chilean flamingo is different from that of the Andean and James' flamingoes, in that the upper mandible is deeper, and the lower shallower, enabling it to feed on very small molluscs living on the bottom of the lakes by sweeping its head from side to side like a vacuum cleaner. The other two species feed on *Aphanocapsa* algae or diatoms nearer the surface. These frequently stain the lakes of the Andes red. The bigger flamingo, the Andean, eats larger organisms than the James', so all three flamingos can feed in the same area without competing with each other.

We were lucky at Surire that there were very large numbers of James' flamingo. Despite being the rarest flamingo in the world it is the commonest on these salt lakes. I estimated that there were some 3500 birds. So Surire must be second only to the Laguna Colorada in Bolivia as a centre for this species, and Surire has not been included in recent flamingo surveys of the Andes. Until 1957 the James' flamingo was believed to be extinct for the simple reason that nobody had been up to these high salt flats to look for it. Zoologically South America is still comparatively unexplored.

Lake Titicaca appears to be shrinking, and one day may also be a salar, but it has a long way to go. It is enormous, considering its altitude of 12,500 feet. It has an area of 3141 square miles and is 1214 feet deep. Such a large body of water has a considerable effect on the climate, which is much milder in the region of the lake, whose waters remain at a more or less constant 11°C. The surrounding Altiplano has always been an important centre for Indian settlement, and indeed one tribe, the Urus, retreated onto its waters, where they live on floating islands made from the totora rushes that grow in thick beds in the shallows at the edge of the lake. These rushes are also used to make the famous balsa rafts which are still used by the Indians for fishing. But apart from these beautiful rafts, the famous steamships and its Inca connections, Lake Titicaca is now an unattractive place.

It is surrounded by a rapidly expanding population which has already hopelessly overgrazed and depleted the poor soil on its shores. The landscape is disfigured by an astonishing number of new corrugated metal roofs which reflect the sun like glass strawberry cloches on a Cornish hillside. Anybody who has slept in a hut with one of these roofs will know how apallingly cold they are compared with thatch. It was impossible for us to film anything other than tracking shots through the reeds on the lake, and we had to go to the nearby

Lago Umayo for our shots of the flightless short-winged grebe.

One of the interesting creatures found in Lake Titicaca is a giant toad which has retreated from the cold and the high rate of evaporation of the air to become totally aquatic. It has a very baggy skin, through which it breathes, as its lungs have almost disappeared. It has well-developed webbed feet and eyes more like those of a fish than an amphibian.

We got our toads from two children who spent the whole night out in their boat fishing, wrapped in blankets. Our film of the reeds went well with the wonderful light and towering cumulus clouds reflected in the lake. We were well on the way to supporting the fallacy that it was an attractive lake.

The weather broke at 2 pm. and as we headed west from Juliaca to cross the western ridge of the Andes towards the coast, we drove towards the blackest sky I can remember. The cloud base hung in folds of deep charcoal grey, pressing down on the treeless landscape. As we breasted the hills that border the Titicaca rift to the west, lightning bolts split the sky. In the gloom Indians were running across the naked plain, smudges of brilliant pinks and mauves, tiny bowler hats held to their heads and children bouncing in shawls on their backs.

The road to Arequipa has an evil reputation. That night we had hail, rain, sleet, snow, fog, mud and finally choking clouds of dust in the desert. We reached our hotel in Arequipa at 3 am. and then had completely to unload a ton of equipment from the vehicles into our rooms as there was no safe place to leave them. But in doing so we found a forgotten crate of beer!

At Cruz del Condor we filmed condors cruising slowly past beneath us. Below them the river Colca surged in a brown torrent of mud and stones, 3600 feet vertically down. Beyond us, on the northern side of the narrow canyon, the mountains vanished up into cloud which parted now and again to reveal a line of snow-clad summits. From those nearby glaciers to the water below us was a vertical drop of 9800 feet. The Grand Canyon in Arizona is 5600 feet deep. It has a wide panorama, but the Colca Canyon is a narrow slit in the hide of the earth. Tourists never see it, but it is one of the wonders of the Andes.

One of the more interesting families of plants native to the Americas is that of the bromeliads. They are characterised by spiky rosettes of fleshy leaves, and are found growing on the branches of trees, on the ground, including the desert, and jutting from rocks. The pineapple is a well-known species of bromeliad, although few people who have not seen it cultivated realise that it grows on top of a rosette of spiky leaves.

Millions of years ago, in clearings in the polylepis woods, a variety of bromeliad developed which is the most impressive flowering plant in the world. There are still a few widely scattered areas of the Altiplano in Peru and Bolivia where the *Puya raimondii* can be found. It is such an ancient plant that it is considered to be a 'living fossil', and it grows extremely slowly. It is usually said that it takes a hundred years to grow, until it forms a large ball of very sharp-pointed, tough, sword-shaped leaves. It then throws out a flower spike which towers to a height of forty-five feet above the bare grassland, an extremely striking spectacle.

The spike is made up of spirals of 400–500 flowering branches, each carrying some fifty greenish-white flowers. Although these bloom in succession from the base of the spike upwards it means that each plant carries some 20,000 flowers, and sets about twelve million seeds. Pollination is carried out by humming-birds which swarm round the flowering plant, perching on the bare extremities of the branches. The giant puya puts all its accumulated resources into the flower spike, and then dies. New plants can be found flowering only about every three years.

Despite the magnificent spectacle they bring to these barren cold lands, and the huge quantity of seeds they set, the plants are dying out, because the Indians set fire to them, burning the dead leaves and also the dry flower-spikes. The reason for this is that the leaves carry along their edges strong curved hooks pointing inwards, which turn the rosettes into traps which can catch lambs and animals as strong as a domestic cat. Even children are at risk.

In a barren landscape the big rosettes of the puya afford valuable shelter from wind and hail to a large variety of birds which build their nests between the spiked leaves. The inward-curving spines hold the nests fast in the fierce winds. But any unguarded movement by the birds can result in them becoming caught by the spines, so that the more they struggle the more they work their way into the centre of the plant. In areas where the plants are undisturbed by the Indians, there can be as many as 14 nests in one plant, but every plant also carries its sad complement of corpses of finches, doves, and even hawks.

There is no doubt that the plants are beneficial to the birds, providing them with a secure nesting area in an inhospitable environment. But is it a genuine bird-eating plant? Because of the high altitude and the fast rate of evaporation the corpses tend to mummify, and if the plant does use them as a source of chemicals, they must be leached out very slowly. Equally, the droppings left on the leaves, sometimes in thick layers, do not appear to be dissolved much. Also the radial form of the leaves causes birds to perch or nest on the lower hemisphere, where water is thrown off by the inclination of the leaves. But if the plant wanted to catch birds, it is well designed for the purpose. At least it is a fascinating possibility that merits further investigation, and is another good reason to preserve these extraordinary relics that stand like great candles in ornate holders on this empty land.

9

Volcanoes on the Equator, Bears, Humming-birds and the Cloud Forest

Every year more than 30,000 tourists come to Ecuador specifically to look at wildlife – but on the Galapagos Islands. Despite the lure of the great volcanoes like Chimborazo and Cotopaxi, that can be seen towering above the clouds from far out at sea, only a tiny fraction of the visitors see anything of the wildlife of the mainland. Nevertheless, Ecuador is an extremely beautiful country with an extraordinarily rich flora and fauna, and it is far more accessible, thanks to the good roads and short distances, than similar riches in Peru or Colombia. As so often in South America, the natural history of the country is largely unknown even to scientists, but it is widely recognised that Ecuador has an outstanding diversity of plants, and of course the plant-life determines the diversity of animal species.

The reason for this wealth of species is the combination of Ecuador's position astride the equator, and the climatic variation brought about by the great height of the Andes, so that almost every climate in the world is represented. This was brought home to me by a walk on the west side of the volcano Pichincha which overlooks the capital, Quito. At 10,000 feet I found myself in a forest of bamboo and ferns with an understorey of *gunnera* that looked just like the Valdivian rain forest we had seen over 3500 miles further south in Chile, an example of altitude having the same effect as latitude on temperature and vegetation. Here swirling cloud replaced the rain of the south and splendidly colourful humming-birds and tanagers gleamed amidst the thick foliage. Yet there was still a relative of the chucao cackling in the bushes, and later we were to see many of the birds we associated with Patagonia: the buff-necked ibis and the torrent duck, and even the dwarf deer, the pudu, high on the slopes that hang above the Amazon forests.

The Andean highlands of Ecuador consist of a series of high basins along a north–south central valley dominated on either side by the famous Avenue of Volcanoes, more than thirty geologically recent peaks. The highest is Chimborazo (20,577 feet), which for a long time was considered to be the highest mountain in the world, and in fact, theoretically, still is, because the equatorial bulge of the earth makes the summit of Chimborazo the point on the earth's surface furthest from its centre. Usually only three of the volcanoes are considered to be active by the guide books, Cotopaxi, Tungurahua, and Sangay, but volcanoes that have not erupted for a few hundred years are by no means always dead, and Antisana, for example (forty miles south-east of Quito), produced a lava flow eight miles long in 1760. There are also several large calderas – collapsed cones of volcanoes – the most spectacular of which is Altar, which has a ruined wall of rock fingers standing above glaciers which tumble down both inside and outside its shattered rim.

When we arrived in Quito it was the centenary of Edward Whymper's successful first ascent of Chimborazo. Nobody saw fit to celebrate this feat by the man who had conquered the Matterhorn, nor his series of first ascents of six of the other great volcanoes, including Cayambe and Antisana, made the same year. On each occasion he and his companions, the two Italian Carrel cousins, carried a heavy mercury barometer to the summit, to establish the height, and often a camera and tripod and other instruments as well. Whymper climbed Chimborazo twice, for good measure, and took a photograph the second time of his party on the summit, enveloped in an ash cloud from an eruption of Cotopaxi that had begun a few hours earlier. He apologised in his book for the poor quality of the photograph.

As Whymper observed, the Ecuadorians had left the exploration of their volcanoes to others. The same could be said about their natural history. Since the visits of La Condamine in 1735–1743, and Humboldt in 1801, almost all significant field work has been carried out by foreigners, all of whom have suffered from the same problems of achieving practical results in a country where show matters more than diligence.

Our hotel, the Intercontinental, was full of bullfighters, flown over – with their bulls – from Spain, but our mini-bus was broken into with the aid of an hotel spoon while locked in the hotel car-park, surrounded by an eight-foot fence. It had taken me two weeks to get it out of the customs. There were two circuses in town, and one night one of their elephants was stolen.

But there were some compensations. When I arrived on my recce my guide complained that he had forgotten to take his beer-bottles back so he didn't have any money for petrol for his jeep. I thought this was rather odd until I discovered I could buy fourteen gallons for a pound ($2.30).

The discovery of oil in the eastern forests has transformed the economy of Ecuador, but it has meant a very rapid introduction of roads and colonisation into an area that even twenty years ago was totally unexplored, an area up until then only known by the nomadic Indian tribes.

From the Gulf of Guayaquil northwards the Andes are no longer a barrier dividing a desert on the west from a jungle on the east. Both sides of the range receive heavy rains and are covered in tropical forest, the narrow central valley has a pleasant moist climate, and the highlands of the western and eastern ranges of the Cordillera are much wetter than the Altiplano of Peru, and are called Páramos. The third film of my series was to follow the Amazon down from the ice-caps of the equator to the lowland flood forest.

Juan Black's grandfather was a colonist from Jamaica but his expansive gestures were South American. We were talking about the east side of the volcano Antisana. I was sitting in a plywood hut that Juan himself had constructed at 14,000 feet on the Páramo of Antisana where he has spent several years studying the ecology, living alone with his wife and children in the immensity of the bleak but beautiful rolling lava plain; a notable exception to my comments about Ecuadorian naturalists. Although only two and a half hours drive from Quito the Páramo is remarkably unspoilt because it is all privately owned, part of an hacienda that the owner believes measures about forty thousand hectares. He is not sure because the eastern side of the mountain has never been mapped. It is only recently that it has had any boundary to the east at all; it formerly extended 'as far as you can go to the east'. It comprises an important reserve of the vanishing fauna of the highlands, as it is the highest hacienda in the country. I was most grateful to the owner for permission to film there, and for the help of his men.

We set up our tents next to Juan's hut in the tufts of calmagrostis and festuca grass. His hut was in the lee of a lava outcrop that protected it from the icy winds that dropped from the 18,717 foot peak of Antisana. We were on the south-western flank, and the view towards the central valley was amazing. A hundred miles away Chimborazo caught the sun, clean and bright against the sky, but before us was the vast conical pile of Cotopaxi. It was twenty-five miles away, yet immense, standing some eight thousand feet above the plateau. From the centre of its crater rose a thin wisp of smoke.

When Cotopaxi erupted in 1877 a froth of incandescent lava poured over the notches in the lip of that crater. A lahar of water, blocks of ice, mud and rock reached Latacunga at a speed of fifty miles an hour, sweeping away buildings and every bridge in its course. Huge blocks of ice were left stranded on the plain thirty miles from the mountain, and some remained for months. Meanwhile the lahar, heading northwards, reached Esmeraldas on the Pacific coast, 150 miles away in a straight line, but more than twice that distance by the route taken. (I find it very curious that Latacunga has been rebuilt repeatedly on its old site.)

A tremendous frieze of cumulus covered the east, but Antisana watched above us against the waking glimmer of Orion lying on its back above the crater. A short-eared owl fanned back and forth across the tuft-grass looking for rodents, and range upon range of grey-mauve hills receded to the west. The moment the sun went down it was bitterly cold.

Before light I was woken by an extraordinary swishing, zipping noise, almost like a jet fighter in the distance. It was the drumming of the Cordilleran snipe. It was a glorious dawn, with Cotopaxi rose-pink against a clear blue sky and hoar-frost sparkling the grasses with blue gems all around us. Now the air rang with the plaintive pipe of the Andean lapwing.

As the first rays of sun fell across the tops of the grasses, Hugh filmed an

Andean hillstar humming-bird on a chuquiraga bush preening and stretching itself as the sun warmed its bones. It seems extraordinary to find humming-birds so high, yet the *Oreotrochilus* genus will nest as high as 15,000 feet. The nests are often sited to catch the first rays of the sun, and are surprisingly large for a humming-bird – no doubt for insulation. Hugh found one nest in a typical site, tucked under an overhang of turf at the top of a bank of lava where the vicious hail of the afternoons could not reach it. One way in which this tiny ball of feathers survives is by letting its body temperature drop at night to only 14°C. from a normal 39.5°C. By reducing its rate of metabolism to as little as one twentieth of the daytime rate it is able to conserve energy and avoid moving to a lower and warmer altitude. The bird becomes torpid in this state, rather as the green-backed firecrown does in winter in Tierra del Fuego, but the longest the Andean hillstar would normally have to survive without feeding is a few days of storm.

In a shallow grassy valley with a view of the snow cap of volcano Cayambe, which has its summit actually on the equator, I watched the ice-crystals melt on the leaves of a mountain lupin. We filmed a little rivulet. It was only six inches across, trickling beneath a hatched fringe of ice needles. Above us the edge of the glacier was beginning to drip. Soon the stream would cloud and grow with the sudden rush of melt waters from the glaciers, and begin its long journey down to the Amazon three miles beneath us. Further down, already a rushing brook, it ran between our tents and Juan's hut where it had cut twenty feet down into the ground forming a small quebrada, exposing on the walls layers of brown and cream like some expensive chocolate cake. These layers, carved full of holes by oven-birds, were ash deposits from the volcanoes that brooded above us. Andean hillstars hawked for insects over the stream. Between the grasses the ground was strewn with flowers – gentians, composites and cushion plants – hugging together for warmth and protection from evaporation. The flowers seemed oddly familiar, and in fact this flora invaded from temperate zones in the north and south as the Andes were raised, rather than the local tropical flora, which is mostly woody, budding off new high-altitude species.

In the wetter areas of the Páramo were dozens of atelopus frogs, their backs jet black to absorb the energy of the sun. The whole ground crawled with them, mostly locked in couples in a nuptial embrace that lasts for weeks on end.

Besides filming the ice-caps, the condors, and the life of the Páramo grasslands, our main reason for going to Antisana was to try to film the spectacled bear and the woolly tapir. Juan Black had assured me that both of these could be found on the eastern side of the mountain where the vegetation was very different, being much wetter than the west. These are two very rare animals, and I knew that they would be extremely difficult to film, but I thought that here we would have as good a chance as anywhere, particularly because we had as our guide one of the peons from the hacienda, Julio Villatuña, who had himself tracked and shot bears (despite the fact that they are protected).

Julio brought up six pack horses from the hacienda below. We had the usual

112

66

PREVIOUS PAGE
Vilcanota valley
montane forest near
Machu Picchu

LEFT Montane forest
near Coca falls

OPPOSITE TOP   Volcano
Antisana with gentians
CENTRE   Green jay
BOTTOM   Espeletias,
Páramo, El Angel

67

68

69

ABOVE Montane forest
below Reventador
volcano
RIGHT Cock of the rock

72

ABOVE Long-tailed
hermit humming-bird of
the lowland rain forest
LEFT Paradise tanager

73

OPPOSITE *and* ABOVE
Amazon lowland rain
forest
OPPOSITE BELOW LEFT
King vulture
BELOW RIGHT
Great egret

RIGHT   Baby caiman
amongst water-
hyacinths

OVERLEAF   Prop-roots of
palms, Amazon rain
forest

ABOVE   Amazon varzéa
flood forest
RIGHT   Piranha

OPPOSITE   Black-water
stream

Three-toed sloth

Night-monkey

87

ABOVE Yellow-headed parrot taking a shower

PREVIOUS PAGE Scarlet and red-and-green macaws on a salt-lick, River Manu

problem: each horse has to be led over rough ground, yet the more people you have the more food you have to carry. As in Chiloé I was very surprised by the loads the small horses could carry over very difficult ground. By cutting our personal belongings to a minimum we managed to get all the tents and equipment onto the six horses. Julio rode ahead with a shot-gun. Both Juan and Julio had emphasised to us the danger of meeting wild bulls on the way. They were descendants of fighting bulls brought from Spain centuries before and had been roaming Antisana wild for generations. When solitary they could be very dangerous.

It was a beautiful clear morning, but it took us until 10.30 to get the loads made up and balanced. We had not been going ten minutes when the first load slipped off and my camera box flew through the air from a kick. But it proved to be the only bad hold-up we had. With the sunshine and the flowers and the wonderful views it was a most stimulating morning. Buff-necked ibises honked overhead, and below us we could see herds of wild cattle to add a spice of danger.

Volcanoes tend to erode into what is called parasol ribbing – they begin to look like a half-collapsed umbrella, with streams eroding steep valleys that run radially down the cone. Since they all tend to look alike they can be very confusing in cloud. It also makes it hard work skirting round a volcano, because one has constantly to climb and descend these diagonal slopes. At first we had only the old lava fields to contend with. Some of these had bogs, betrayed by clusters of very green hummock plants, and we had to cross them with care. But as we worked higher to 15,500 feet we were in wet grassland and the going got harder. There was a keen wind, and cloud began to condense around us. I found my breath was short, despite having been living at 9000 feet for some weeks. I was very glad not to be carrying a pack, and even pulling a reluctant horse became a strain. We crossed some icy streams, white with lava dust, and climbed a long slope until we topped a ridge and a great amphitheatre opened before us with a fine thin waterfall plunging down from the ice above on our left. There was a choice of routes here; either we could skirt the bottom of a vertical cliff, or we could go diagonally down the steep slope below us, and climb again at an angle the five hundred feet or so that we had lost. But Julio said the upper trail was very narrow and if a horse caught its load on the cliff it would fall to its death. There were swamps in the bottom of the valley but as Julio pointed out, if a horse fell there at least it would not be killed. So down we went. My good boots had been stolen in Quito and I continually slipped on the cushion plants and fell. The grass was soaking wet and we were wearing rubberised canvas ponchos and waterproof trousers, excellent local garments, but striped rather like sickly brown pyjamas.

We slipped and floundered our way down, and found a place to ford the river. A huge brown bull watched us from on top of a big rock – the lord of the valley. Then the horses sank to their bellies in the swamp. It was a tiring and dangerous business getting them out, but we got them clear and tramped on up the slope. The tussock-grass concealed deep clefts and it was hard to tell what was firm and what was not for the heavily laden horses. My legs ached and my back was wet with sweat despite the wind, but the going could have been a lot worse.

Then we topped another ridge and the cloud parted to reveal a view that made the whole hard walk worthwhile. In front the wide flat stony bed of the river Azufre sloped down towards the right where it disappeared into a dark steep gorge overgrown with forest – the valley of the river Quijos. Clumps of polylepis forest clung to both sides of the valley, and to the left a thin white cascade fell hundreds of feet down from a deep notch cut in the top of a cliff that faced us. Above it reared six thousand feet of ice and rock half-veiled in cloud. Three fine bulls watched us from the river and then moved off into the bush opposite.

Beyond the slope in front of us nobody ever ventured, Julio assured us, and we did not doubt him. And beyond the Quijos to the right was also unknown territory of trackless woods and alpine meadows. We slid and stumbled down a last long incline, and made a comfortable camp under the cliff at the head of the valley, well hidden amongst the polylepis trees. So far things had gone better than I had expected, and certainly I had not expected to find such a good hidden camp site on the side of the mountain. We were at 12,500 feet.

Over supper we discussed with Julio what he knew about the spectacled bears. Only two months before, he had come this way to hunt on a bank holiday. Just where our horses had so nearly got stuck he had shot at a white-tailed deer, and a bear had rushed away from nearby cover. Some months earlier he had disturbed another bear and it had run away across the valley where we now were camped. On a third occasion further down towards the Quijos canyon he had seen a mother with two cubs playing and he had tried to shoot the mother to catch the cubs. He described how when he had shot at the mother bear, another bear had jumped out of the bushes only twenty feet ahead of him, and had tucked its head between its legs and rolled down the hill like a ball. Most of what Julio told us was found to be accurate and there was no reason why he should have made this up.

Julio continued disarmingly that bears tasted like pork, but that it was difficult to get them home as no horse would carry a bear carcase. He had also killed two bears a few years previously on another part of the mountain. It was not encouraging to hear that the bears had been shot at. We did our best to persuade him not to kill them in the future. But Julio also told us that being curious, they would rise on their hind legs to get a better view if they were not frightened. We decided that the best plan was to avoid disturbance as much as possible, and to keep a look-out over the valley from a promontory of rock near the camp.

After breakfast I climbed a rise behind the camp, and a few minutes later found a puya plant (a smaller species than the *Puya raimondii* of Peru) which was freshly torn open at the base. It seemed remarkable that anything could eat those rosette plants with their dagger-like leaves edged with vicious spines, but a bear had ripped the centre out and eaten the base of the leaves just as we might eat a globe artichoke. There was a neat pile of chewed leaves to the left and I could even see where the bear had stood. Julio said it was three days old, but many others had been eaten in the area earlier. We were certainly in the right spot.

Hugh and I watched the valley with binoculars all morning, searching methodically up and down the slopes but saw nothing more interesting than a black-chested buzzard eagle being mobbed by a caracara. Donaldo went with Julio down the right-hand side of the valley towards the gorge to investigate a track that Julio knew. They followed it through thick cover where it was no more than a tunnel, and over very steep ground. The bears were clearly good at scrambling around cliffs. They found fresh tracks, the rear print like that of a child, and the fore-print like that of a puma. There was more recently eaten puya, and they could even smell the bear, but they saw nothing in the thick cover.

In the afternoon we again watched from our vantage-point as Donaldo and Julio explored the next valley to the east. Donaldo reported that it would be hopeless for filming. You can't hope to film an animal that you come on at close range by surprise, as it takes so long to set the camera up. Even if you do get a shot the chances are that you will see only the rear of the retreating animal. We seemed to be in the best place but we were concerned at the amount of disturbance we had caused nearby. The three big bulls had not reappeared, and if they were scared to return the bears might be also. The cloud swept in from the east and in the afternoon it rained.

It was cold and wet in camp and it was almost impossible to get a fire to burn up because of the lack of air, but the next day dawned clear. Julio had to leave as he had to vote in the local provincial elections. If he did not he would be fined a month's pay. He said he had no idea who he was going to vote for. Then half way through the morning he returned, making our hearts leap when we saw a movement on the hill. He had seen two white-tailed deer and had come back to tell us. We decided to watch only from the knoll to try to keep the valley quiet for two days. We began to pick out the puyas that had been eaten and a path where the bears had pushed through the grass. We took it in turns to watch for two hours. Even in the drizzle it was pleasant to sit half-hidden on the knoll with a commanding view of the whole valley, watching the colours in the flowers and the trees, and the grandeur of the cliffs and waterfall. All the same, there was very little life of any kind: a humming-bird came within a couple of feet as it fed on the blossom of a bush, whilst an antpitta called in a melancholy descending scale of three notes. I found my powers of observation increasing with practice, and I don't think we missed anything.

One major problem was that we knew so little about the bear's habits, despite having been in contact with Bernard Peyton, an American who had been studying them in the wild in Peru since 1977. The spectacled bear is so-called because of the variable pattern of light bands around its face on a dark brown or black coat. It is a small bear, the male weighing up to 140 kilos, but the female only half that amount. It is probably the least known of all the bear family, though it has been bred in captivity since 1949. It is thought to range through the Andes from western Venezuela to Bolivia, and in Peru Peyton found bear traces in a wide range of habitats from coastal scrub desert at only 650 feet above sea level, to Páramo at 13,600 feet. It has always been a prize for big-game hunters, and many used to be shot on their annual migrations to the desert floodplains in Peru, but they have not been seen there for fifteen years.

Ironically, however, it is not hunters but the handing over in Peru of the big estates to the local population that threatens its future most. As in the case of the vicuña, the invasion of the countryside since the military government of 1968 expropriated the large estates has destroyed large areas of bear habitat and caused crops to be planted for the first time in areas where bears will come to eat them, and get shot for the damage they cause. Only in the precipitous cloud forest, like that at the end of our valley, are they safe, but it is a habitat that they seldom use, because they prefer more open ground.

That evening Hugh spotted a condor coming in to roost on the cliff above our camp. There was already another one perched on the ledge. They were both immature, perhaps four years old, with brown feathers but the beginning of the white ring. They bowed facing each other and began to peck at each other's neck feathers. Probably they were beginning courting behaviour. Condors are shy creatures on the ground, and it cheered me that they did not find us a disturbance. But we were becoming disheartened at seeing no sign of the bears.

The following day was Sunday and it rained. By nine when the cloud lifted the condors had gone, but Hugh spotted a chewed puya that had not been eaten the day before. This seemed to confirm our worst suspicions, that the bears were feeding at night. We had been told that they made nests in the bushes or trees to sleep at night so this was a new and disturbing piece of evidence. We had another blank day.

The following afternoon Juan arrived with his wife and Julio. We went with him over the ridge opposite to look at the site where he had seen the woolly or mountain tapir. We saw its dung on a track on the way, and there was a clearing by a stream below, where I thought we might get a shot of it in the morning. Even less is known about the woolly tapir than the spectacled bear but we were able to add nothing. The following day the cloud was low and it showed no signs of lifting so we packed up camp and started back. We had no more time.

We had spent a week in a wet camp with nothing to show for it. The disappointment was worst for Hugh. They were the first animals he had ever failed to film. However, Peyton himself saw only six bears in fifty-four field trips.

One of the strangest of all the unexpected sights of the Andes are the Páramos covered with espeletia plants: cold rolling misty moorlands sprouting with what looks like mutant cabbages, or an invasion of triffids; rosette-trees, up to five metres high, related to the sunflower and dandelion. The silvery-green furry leaves which sprout like a bouquet from the top of the thick stems wither and hang down, shrouding the stems with a tapering matted muff which makes them look startlingly like human figures when seen from a distance in the mist. This has brought them their local name of *frailejones*, or greyfriars.

Despite the fact that they grow on peat, in an atmosphere of almost permanent mist, the leaves are designed to conserve moisture and reflect excessive light, for when the sky does clear, the equatorial light is intense. We were lucky enough to visit the Páramo del Angel when black thunder-clouds parted to allow sun to strike the plants in the foreground, and they looked intensely dramatic. The area was alive with rabbits, and a good number of culpeo foxes in pursuit.

Probably the most remarkable group of birds found exclusively in the Americas are the humming-birds. They reach their greatest diversity in the temperate and sub-tropical forests of the Andes, and in Ecuador there are at least one hundred and twenty-nine species. Even in the garden of our hotel in Quito we were able to film several beautiful varieties including the spectacular black-tailed trainbearer which has an enormously long twin tail. There are few sights in nature more delightful than to watch a humming-bird work over the blossoms of a flowering shrub, or take a bath in a sunlit shower. Curiously the pigment tints of the feathers are only black and rufous, the most basic colours, and most of the colours of the plumage depend on refraction of light. This is why they only show when the light hits them at the right angle. It also gives them their jewel-like brilliance.

Francisco Pizarro described the humming-bird feathers for the Inca emperor which the Conquistadors found in Cusco. 'There were deposits of iridescent feathers, some looking like fine gold and others of a shining green colour . . . each feather is little larger than a fingernail. Quantities of them were threaded together on fine thread and were skillfully attached to agave fibres to form pieces over a span in length. These were all stored in leather chests. Clothes were made of the feathers, and contained a staggering quantity of these iridescents. There were many other feathers of various colours intended for making clothing to be worn by the lords and ladies at the festivals . . .'

Humming-birds are very light, weighing from 2 to 20 grams, and they have a very high rate of metabolism. This means that they must feed frequently – not just on nectar from flowers, but on proteins from insects. Many insects are caught within the flowers, but it is quite common to see humming-birds catch insects in the air.

No other bird can match their manoeuverability, which comes from their method of flight. Instead of beating their wings up and down like other birds, they beat them to and fro in a shallow figure of eight. First the lower and then the upper surface tilts downwards and pushes the air down. This means that by altering the tilt of the wings the bird can make a quick transition from forward flight to hovering and even flying backwards. Insects such as flies move their wings the same way. It is the high speed of the humming-birds' wings, up to 80 beats a second, that causes the 'hum'. They can also fly at up to 70 miles per hour, and some north American species fly very long distances. The rufous humming-bird breeds in Alaska and migrates to South America for the winter. It is not surprising that the breast muscles of a humming-bird account for a third of its total weight.

Humming-birds in the tropics frequently have territories containing a food supply which they defend fiercely and bad-temperedly against intruders, stabbing with their bills at other humming-birds and even at birds as large as hawks. This specialisation on a particular food supply has led to an interesting co-evolution between birds and plants. As the humming-bird sips nectar through its long hollow tongue, it picks up pollen which it carries to the next flower to pollinate it. Both flowers and birds have adapted to suit one another. The sword-bill humming-bird has a bill as long as its body and tail which is adapted to probe the long tube-like passion flower *Passiflora mixta* and the deep bells of the datura species. The white-tipped sicklebill has a bill curved into a quarter-circle so that it can sit on a heliconia flower and reach up to dip its bill into the one above.

We watched a giant humming-bird – the size of a swift – defending a flowering tree from flower-piercers, a family of small birds with a sharp bill crossed at the tip like secateurs, which steals nectar from the bell-shaped flowers by nipping the base of the flower where the nectar collects, drinking it as it leaks to the outside. But at the same time other humming-birds were taking advantage of the holes made by the flower-piercers to reach into flowers which were too deep for the length of their bills! We were beginning to witness the complexity of relationships which is the hallmark of the tropical forest. The flowers' nectar is to attract a pollinator, but the flower-piercers were beating the system.

The Quijos river whose birth we had witnessed at the glaciers of Antisana changes its name to the Coca river as it plunges steeply through the cloud forest of the eastern slopes of the Cordillera. But just when it should be entering the Amazon lowlands a volcano rears to the north. Reventador (11,434 feet) stands well to the east of the other volcanoes of Ecuador, and is one of the most active. Yet despite the fact that the oil pipeline from Lago Agrio to Quito curls round the forest-clad cliffs at the base of its cone, it is very little known, partly because it is almost continually obscured by cloud. It was a new experience after the open expanse of the Páramo to see this ashy peak standing clear above the thick tangle of the forest, smoking gently in the sunset. The ground around it is extremely precipitous, with vertical canyons and cliffs of pumice and basalt hung with a thick mat of ferns, and trees covered with aerial gardens of bromeliads, mosses and orchids, all the more luxuriant for being fertilised by the phosphate in the ash from Reventador. Some time in the past an eruption filled the Coca valley, and now the river surges through a canyon and plunges over a fall 475 feet high. We chose this splendid setting to film the montane rain forest and its brilliant birds.

The eastern slopes of the Andes form some of the most spectacular and inaccessible habitats in the world. Anyone who has visited the fortified Inca town of Machu Picchu, with its superb views of the river Urubamba snaking round the rocky pedestal on which it stands, will know how steep the mountains of the montane rain forest can be. They may also have seen fires running away out of control up the mountainsides, caused by peasant farmers who have settled in the valley. So far there is only a railway, but a road is due to come, and roads bring settlement and destruction in their wake. Four and a half million acres of tropical rain forest on the eastern Andean slopes have been destroyed by shifting agriculture in Peru in the last thirty years, a very substantial proportion of the total. Yet there are many areas like the Pantiacolla range which have never been explored, and are still reputed to hold lost Inca cities, and certainly are the home of uncontacted Indian tribes. In Ecuador, with less population pressure, the damage is less and there are still magnificent areas east of the great volcanoes which are so inaccessible, due to the steepness of the slopes, that they may remain the last places to be explored on the globe. Anybody who has tried to climb the vertical rain-swept cliffs and deep chasms filled with dripping vegetation will understand why.

This is the home of the cock-of-the-rock, one of the most famous of all the South American birds. About the size of a jackdaw, it is remarkable for the male's brilliant orange or red colouring and a semi-circular crest which crowns its head and almost hides its bill. Alfred Russel Wallace gives a good description of the difficulty of reaching its terrain:

'We toiled on, now climbing by roots and creepers up perpendicular walls, now creeping along a narrow ledge, with a yawning chasm on each side of us. I could not have imagined such serrated rocks to exist. It appeared as if a steep mountain side had been cut and hacked by some gigantic force into fissures and ravines, from fifty to a hundred feet deep . . . and through the dense forest and matted underwood, with which every part of these rocks were covered, we could see an interminable succession of ridges, and chasms, and gigantic blocks of stone, with no visible termination.' He collected twelve skins, but all were lost, along with the whole of his collection from four years in the jungle, when his ship caught fire on his way back across the Atlantic. It was Wallace who, during an attack of fever in the Molucca Islands, had the inspiration that natural selection was the driving force behind evolution. He wrote at once to Darwin who had come to the same conclusion, and prompted their famous joint communication to the Linnean Society on the theory of evolution.

The nineteenth century was the great age of collectors, and the rubber and nitrate booms drew attention as never before to South America. The wealthy had their tropical orchid houses and giant Amazonian water-lilies, the middle classes their temperate monkey-puzzle trees and conservatories. There was a fashion for cases of humming-birds in the drawing room, and women wore them on their hats. Even naturalists as fine as Darwin and Wallace would, on seeing an interesting animal, immediately try to secure a specimen – in other words, to kill it, rather than watch what it did. In consequence, species became well known, though almost nothing was known of their habits. There are few creatures more conspicuous than a cock-of-the-rock, and its beauty, allied to the remoteness and difficulty of the country in which it lived, ensured that it was a frequent target: a valuable specimen for the hunter who made his living collecting them. By the time the skin reached England, it had become a bird that sat around on rocks in an open landscape and behaved more like a black grouse than a fruit-eating bird of the forest. There was also a strange report that it danced.

The connection with rocks was accurate, in that the female birds build mud nests on cliffs, but it was not until 1961 that the dance was first observed in detail by a scientist in Guiana. Each male clears a little patch on the forest floor about two or three feet across, removing fallen leaves and even stripping bark off roots. The males descend to their 'courts' and fan their wings and bob and click their bills to try to lure a female down to mate with them. David Snow described to me how in 1970 he had seen, once, a female come down to a court and begin to nibble at the male's wing feathers which are modified into long silky fringes. Unfortunately, in trying to take a photograph, he scared the female away; but it was almost certainly a prelude to mating.

So far I have described the Guianan cock-of-the-rock which occurs along the north side of the Amazon basin in an arc from the Guianas to eastern Colombia. The species that we wished to film was the Andean one which is slightly less brilliant, with small differences of colour pattern and form of the crest. It occurs from north-west Venezuela to Bolivia, and in Ecuador there are two sub-species: on the west of the Andes the males are brilliant red; the males on the east are more orange. Both forms live in dense montane forest.

Cocks-of-the-rock are much easier to see than their reputation would have us believe. Besides the Coca Falls there were three sites in Peru that I knew of, including one near the railway station for Machu Picchu! I had chosen the Coca Falls as it allowed us the opportunity for general filming of the montane forest as well, rather than making a specific journey just for the cock. There we were lucky to get a shot – albeit in swirling mist – of an umbrella bird displaying its extraordinary black crest like an extravagant plume on a helmet, and inflating its huge dangling feather-covered wattle. This is perhaps the first time that it had been filmed. But so far as the cock-of-the-rock was concerned, it was far from ideal.

The first evening we arrived we saw them, high up beneath the thick canopy of a tree, and it was soon clear, as our stay lengthened, that this was a favourite perch, and indeed they displayed there. In 1959 Ecuador had produced a stamp illustrating the cock-of-the-rock in its old pose on a rock with the mountains behind. As we guessed, this was simply perpetuating the collectors' error. Here they were, sure enough, in thick forest. The problem was that between their favourite tree and the nearest camera position there was a vertical-sided chasm cut in the pumice rock about 30 metres deep, and their tree was over 60 metres from the camera. Once or twice we saw them fly in the open, singly, or in groups, but most of the time they spent fluttering around deep in the shade of the tree. Hugh twice saw a forest falcon perched nearby, and the second time it tried to take one of the cocks, scattering the whole group of half a dozen or so birds. With such brightly coloured plumage they were too obvious a target for birds of prey to be able to sit around in the light, and they kept to the shadows. Up in the canopy the males would stand on a branch and bow down to each other in pairs in a rhythmical pendulum-like fashion with crest erect and back curved; then they would ruffle their black wing-feathers and display their silvery-grey inner secondaries. They would jump through 180 degrees to reverse their position on the branch and jump from branch to branch, always beneath the foliage. We noticed that they seemed to prefer particular perches about six metres above the ground. While they were displaying they also made a most inelegant strangled croaking noise, and when they flew their feathers rattled. Although Hugh finally got some closer shots from the ridge beneath the tree, we never saw them come down to the ground. Nor could I find on the ground any of the leks, as the courts cleared of leaves are called.

We left feeling most disappointed that we had failed to film their lekking display. It was not until I got back to England that I discovered a new study had been made of the Andean cock-of-the-rock in Colombia which showed that they did not lek on the ground, but on horizontal branches in trees. What we had filmed was, after all, the challenge display when two males are contesting their supremacy. Although there is forty percent more light in montane forest than in lowland rain forest, there is still very little, and Hugh did well to get the shots that he did.

Why the two species of cock-of-the-rock should have totally different displays is an intriguing puzzle, especially considering that the males' display plumage is so similar. It is also puzzling that they should have the brilliant plumage at all if it attracts predators. Darwin believed that such extravagant male adornment had been selected for by females preferring to mate with the most showy males. Wallace did not believe this, and the debate goes on, chiefly for lack of any direct evidence that females do select males with discernibly different adornments. Yet this is a bit like Anglo-Saxons saying that all Chinese men look alike. One thing does seem clear. The extraordinary amount of time spent by lekking birds such as the cock-of-the-rock in consorting with their male competitors and competing for the females is possible because they are fruit-eating birds and can feed easily and quickly. Nor do they have to spend time defending their food source. The males are thus 'emancipated' from nest duties, as the female can both incubate and feed quickly. This leaves the males free to display all the year round.

A more complex puzzle about bird colouration concerns the 'radiation' of different kinds of a basically similar species such as the brilliantly coloured tanagers which whirred through the tree tops at the Coca Falls – everybody's idea of what a tropical bird should look like! Finch-like fruit and insect eaters, there are in Ecuador twenty-seven species of the genus Tangara alone. Both sexes are clothed in a riot of colours, varying according to the species which appear to have very similar habits. The function of their brilliant apparel remains a mystery.

10

The Past and Future of the Amazon Rain-Forest

Until quite recently the only way to reach Iquitos, 2,300 miles up the Amazon, was to travel for ten days upstream in a steamer. Now most people first see the Amazon rain forest from the air. There is still no road to Iquitos, thank goodness, but there are daily flights from Miami, and the Peruvian merchants who have grown prosperous on the proceeds of selling Honda motorbikes or pillaging tropical fish, dream of the delights of Disneyland and smuggling cocaine. In Brasilia I had joined a plane-load of middle-income families flying to that greater Amazon city Manaus, set in the heart of the river basin, to buy duty-free colour TV sets. The Amazon is changing fast.

From 33,000 feet the forest was a hazy blue-green, thickly scattered with cotton-wool clouds. So even is that blue carpet of foliage that through half-closed eyes it looked like the sky turned upside down. On the horizon the cumulus towered into the stratosphere as if a broom had swept the cotton wool into a huge ridge, and every few minutes another river slid smoothly beneath with sandbanks gleaming on its looping bends. Twenty minutes at 550 miles an hour and not a sign of Man, then a spark resolved into a tin roof in a clearing – no sign of a road or track. Then a tiny rectangle appeared alone and unheralded, a strip of lighter green at either end. I remembered flying in to one of those rectangles fifteen years before, and my palms sweated with the thought of the landing we made. I had flown out three days later with enough gold from the streams for my wedding-rings, leaving without regret the shanty town and the six-guns and the whores.

A highway, as straight as the line the engineer drew on the map, dull red as dried blood, came in sight. It did not seem to belong. Then, it had taken me six weeks to travel by canoe up the Tapajos, cutting portages round rapids, living on fish and rice. Now it can be driven in a couple of days. Then, the locals had said I would never make it to the headwaters of the River Arinos. Then I travelled on the fringes of the great unknown, camping on islands to be safe from the Indians. Now those neat red lines have split the vastness into fragments and the forest is vanishing before we have learned even half its secrets.

The 'Green Hell' has always bred tall stories; fable has always been hard to separate from fact. But even the facts of the Amazon rain forest can be hard to swallow. There *are* butterflies bigger than some monkeys, dragonflies that catch humming-birds, fish that climb trees. Better knowledge of the jungle provides more not fewer surprises, and it's only in the last decade that our knowledge has moved significantly forward from that of Bates and Wallace, a hundred years ago.

The Amazon is now considered to be the longest river in the world. At 4,168 miles, it is fifty miles longer than the Nile. It drains an area almost as big as the USA (less Alaska), and the rain forest extends across 1.6 million square miles. Two tributaries, the Negro and the Madeira, each carry more water than the Congo. The only other comparable areas of rain forest are in the Malay archipelago, but the Amazon forest is seven and a half times the size of Borneo. Marajó Island in its mouth is larger than Denmark. Discounting the rapidly growing cities like Manaus and Santarem, the Amazon basin, which is the richest area, ecologically, in the world, has as few people per square mile as the Sahara desert.

The Amazon lies just south of the equator, so its tributaries flow from both northern and southern hemispheres and flood at different seasons, and the flow of water is maintained year round. There are seventeen tributaries more than a thousand miles long, and some of them form immense lake-like waterways where they join the main stream. The Tapajos, for example, is thirteen miles across where it joins the Amazon 500 miles from the sea, yet it has a rise and fall of ten to twelve feet in its rainy season. The quantities of water flowing are barely comprehensible, yet this is only the visible part; nearly all the rain that falls on the forest is re-evaporated. It is only a very small proportion that flows to the sea.

Until recently Amazonia was thought to be clothed with a primeval forest that had existed continuously for 300 million years or more, and that it was its age and the constancy of its climate that had given birth to its amazing number of different species of plants and animals and the complexity of the relationships between them. But suddenly a revolutionary and exciting new theory has completely overthrown the old idea of a stable tropical cradle of evolution. Ancient it may be, indeed it is possible that flowering plants first developed in this region, but the great extent of tropical rain forest seen by Francisco Orellana in 1541 has only existed in the last few thousand years. Orellana was the first man to lead an expedition down the Amazon when he was swept away downstream from Gonzalo Pizarro's starving force which had set out from Quito in search of El Dorado. It took him eight months to reach the Atlantic.

Some 250 to 300 million years ago, most of what is now the Amazon basin lay beneath the sea on the edge of the super-continent Pangaea. Rivers flowed towards the west from ancient crystalline rock formations in what are now the Guianas and central Brazil. These built up sediments which slowly drove back the Pacific until about two hundred million years ago the Andes first began to rise. When the west-flowing rivers were cut off from the sea a huge lake formed in the centre of the South American continent, this was filled with sediments and finally the water running off the Andes broke through the ancient rocks of the Atlantic coast to find a new way out to the east and the Amazon came into being. The inias, primitive dolphins, which today swim through the flooded forests, were probably once residents of the western coastal bay.

This complex history means that Amazon tributaries flow from three totally different kinds of soil, and look completely different. From the Guiana and Brazilian shields drain 'clear-water' rivers that are pure and free from minerals. They are acidic and poor in nutrients because any useful chemicals in the rocks from which they rise have long since been leached away by the tropical rains. The second group rise in the sediments which formed in the bed of the former lake system. Beneath a forest which may be a hundred feet high is sand, pure white because even the iron oxides have been leached out. The sand does not bind and break down the tannin in the leaves of the trees in the way that a clay soil can, so the tannin runs off making the streams and rivers a dark tea-colour – in fact they even taste of tea. Because of the lack of nutrients and oxygen in the water and their absorbtion of light, these tributaries are even more infertile than the 'clear-water' rivers. The vegetation has been described as a forest growing on a desert and it is a mystery how the forest managed to establish itself in the first place. There are similar white-sand forests in Borneo called kerangas (meaning 'land on which you cannot grow rice'). It gives some idea of the enormous size of the Amazon basin to compare the Rio Negro – the greatest 'black-water' river – which is two and a half miles wide and 300 feet deep where it joins the main river at Manaus, with the broadest Asian 'black-water' rivers which seldom are as much as sixty feet across.

The third group of tributaries are those that rise in the Andes, frequently carving their way through deep gorges, which twenty years ago were a formidable barrier to travel, but are now becoming playgrounds for adventurous tourists. These 'white-water' rivers are really coffee-with-milk coloured, and are laden with sediments from the Andes which include valuable nutrients. Sometimes they are as thick as liquid mud, and their turbidity and high rate of flow discourage plankton and plant growth in the rivers themselves. However, during the flood seasons, they deposit layers of sediment on the *várzea* flood plain either side of the stream and are an extremely important source of nutrients.

It is not an exaggeration to say that a large proportion of the life of the Amazon rain forest exists because of the recent sediments brought down from the Andes. The influence of the Cordillera is felt far out across the Amazon basin.

One of the greatest misconceptions about the Amazon rain forest is the idea that it is uniform. To an untrained eye it certainly looks uniform from the air, but in reality it is a mosaic of dozens of different kinds of forest on different soils, with different climates, and different species. Even in areas with similar vegetation, animal populations may be different because there are many species which cannot cross rivers, either because they cannot swim long distances (even at Iquitos the Amazon is $3\frac{1}{2}$ miles wide) or because they shun sunlight. Cutting a road can isolate a population of light-fearing birds as effectively as a river.

Most of the other great misunderstandings have come about through a simple lack of knowledge. At first it was thought that any area that could maintain rich tropical forest must be extremely fertile. In fact the forest for the most part works on an extremely efficient closed cycle: the nutrients are almost all bound up in the vegetation and animal life above ground. As leaves are shed they are rapidly decomposed and the minerals reabsorbed by root systems that invade the thin leaf litter itself. Very little is wasted to the rivers. But take away the forest and there is little left. Nevertheless, the reports of the infertility of Amazonian soils were exaggerated. They were based on a very small sample and it is now recognised that they are no more infertile than tropical forest soils in Asia. They are still fragile, and must be treated with care, but the original data was biased by the views of Brazilian scientists who were used to the ultra-fertile soils of São Paulo.

Lack of data is still a major problem in making any assessment of the ecology of the Amazon. In the past botanical, animal and soil collections have been made mostly from those parts of the forest that were easily accessible, the edges of the rivers and near airports. Our knowledge is still woefully inadequate, but it is beginning to expand. The most important new information has come as a result of the Radam survey of Brazilian Amazonia made between 1973 and 1977. The large degree of cloud cover had previously made aerial photographic surveys inadequate, but this was a survey using oblique radar which cuts through cloud to give a picture of the vegetation and the underlying rivers. Supported by false-colour photography, which reveals vegetation types, and ground surveys of sample areas, the data occupy eighteen volumes. The first analysis is shortly to be published, and the results are quite startling.

As recently as 1977 scientists held that 98% of the Amazon rain forest was *Terra firme* or dry-land forest unaffected by seasonality of rains or floods, the variety of forest that has the greatest quantity of growth (biomass). The Radam survey of Brazilian Amazonia shows that dry-land forest comprises only 53% of the total. Within the same climatic conditions there is three or four times as much forest on white sand soils than was realised (6.7%). The two other largest groups are tropical seasonal forest (13.4%), a transitional forest between rain forest and dryer forest, and a combination of savanna with savanna forest (10.3%). Secondary forest and cleared agricultural areas account for 3.9%.

Within the transitional forest two completely new kinds of forest have been recognised: bamboo forest and liana forest. The bamboos climb with the support of a small number of species of *Terra firme* trees to the canopy thirty metres up where they spread to a crown ten metres in diameter. This forest dominates large areas of the State of Acre which once formed part of Bolivia. The liana forest is an open forest with well-spaced trees completely entwined by lianas which are so abundant that it is impossible to walk through the forest without cutting through the tangled stems. It covers large areas between the rivers Tapajós, Xingu and Tocantins, as well as small patches in Roraima and southern Peru. It has never been studied in detail.

It is important to realise that what is unknown scientifically is not necessarily unknown to the local population. An example is the castanha jacaré, a common and useful timber tree well known to the trade in Manaus. As it belongs to a little-studied plant family it was only 'discovered' by science and named *Corythophora rimosa* in 1974. There must be an immense quantity of information quite unsuspected by science which is familiar to local inhabitants, and especially to the indigenous Indians.

It has become a standard generalisation that the idea of impenetrable 'jungle' is not borne out in practise, and that thick growth is only found along the edge of rivers where there is plenty of light. Both the 'new' kinds of forest are impossible to penetrate without a machete.

The most remarkable new information about the forest, however, concerns its history. For a long time it has been realised that a most important characteristic of the forest is its diversity. As Wallace wrote: 'If the traveller notices a particular species and wishes to find more like it, he may often turn his eyes in vain in every direction. Trees of varied forms dimensions and colour are around him, but he rarely sees any one of them repeated. Time after time he goes towards a tree which looks like the one he seeks, but a closer examination proves it to be distinct. He may at length, perhaps, meet with a second specimen half a mile off, or may fail altogether, till on another occasion he stumbles on one by accident.' Expressed in figures, a typical hectare of Amazon forest may contain up to 179 species of trees. The same area of temperate forest would contain only six.

Within the last ten years four groups of biologists, working independently, have discovered that within Amazonia there are some areas richer in species diversity than elsewhere. Data for plants, birds, butterflies and lizards coincide to a remarkable degree with new geological findings. Together they support the revolutionary theory that there have been markedly dry periods in the history of Amazonia with vast fluctuations in the vegetation of the area. These relate to the periods of glaciation nearer the poles. The last glaciation reached its maximum about 18,000 years ago, and with the lowering of the oceans and reduction in rainfall the Amazon rain forest is thought to have retreated to the centres of diversity found today. Forest cover is determined first by rainfall and its seasonality, and to a lesser degree by soil, and it has been found that the highest genetic diversity relates to areas with a mosaic of dense forest around water-courses and open forest on higher rolling ground. When these centres were isolated from one another, species continued to evolve. Later, as the ice retreated and the climate became wetter, they spread out to overlap in areas which had been open, or lower types of forest or savanna.

It is interesting that there are still areas of savanna in high rainfall areas in Venezuela which now contain populations of animals like the South American rattlesnake which cannot cross areas of rain forest. Once these must have been joined. In other areas the rain forest is still slowly advancing.

These new findings are crucial, not just to our understanding of rain forest ecology, but to the future of Amazonia, for it becomes of paramount importance to preserve the centres of diversity or 'refuges'. It has also emphasised the importance of the transitional forest, comprising a fifth of the Amazon basin, which is very little known and is being destroyed faster than any other kind.

Around the world something like 60 thousand square miles – comparable with the area of England and Wales – of tropical forest are being destroyed every year. There is a real possibility that by the time our children grow up there will be no tropical forest left, unless it is protected in reserves.

Usually it has been considered only as something to be exploited for short-term profit as its human history shows.

When Francisco Orellana sailed down the Napo and joined the main stream of the Amazon a little below the modern site of Iquitos he was starving, his sixty men reduced to eating the soles of their shoes cooked with herbs. But soon they began to pass tribe after tribe of prosperous settled Indians who at first welcomed them with food. He noted one village which stretched for six miles along the bank of the river, and another day they passed twenty villages as they drifted downstream. Besides having a plentiful supply of cultivated tropical vegetables and fruits some of the Indian tribes reared turtles and others dried fish. Below the Rio Negro the expedition began to hear of the women warriors who gave the river its name. They were shown feather cloaks and huts full of feathers to be sent as tribute, and somewhere between the Madeira and the Tapajós they passed the gleaming white villages of 'the excellent land and dominion of the Amazons'.

Elsewhere Orellana had been impressed by the glazed pottery which his men considered to be the finest in the world, 'thin and smooth, glazed and with colours shading off into one another in the style of that made in China'.

It is commonly thought that the Amazon rain forest is able only to support small groups of hunter-gatherer Indians, who perhaps supplement their diet with slash-and-burn agriculture on small plots. Orellana's descriptions suggest that there was a considerable settled population along the banks of many of the large rivers with a technically sophisticated culture. It was the advent of the European that drove them from these fertile *várzea* lands, and if they were unable to retreat to the most inaccessible parts of the headwaters of rivers, whole tribes ceased to exist. It is a terrible fact that in the first fifty-seven years of this century eighty-seven entire tribes were destroyed in Brazil. Nothing speeds their end faster than the construction of roads.

When Wallace returned to England in 1859, having spent eleven years collecting in Amazonia, he brought back 14,712 species, no less than 8000 of them new to science. His collection included 14,000 species of insects, and has yet to be surpassed. At about this time the famous rubber-boom began to get under way, spurred on by the invention of vulcanisation and the pneumatic tyre. As the price of raw rubber rose to £1 sterling per pound weight, thousands and thousands of *seringueiros*, or rubber tappers moved into the Amazon and travelled into its furthest backwaters, frequently murdering or enslaving the

Guallatiri volcano and a
high-altitude swamp,
Lauca park, Chile

RIGHT   La Poruna
volcano, a scoria cone
only 300 feet high but
standing at 12,500 feet
on the Puna

ABOVE   Near Ollague,
on the border between
Chile and Bolivia, a
volcano rises above an
ignimbrite plain strewn
with lava outcrops

Cotopaxi volcano from our camp at 14,000 feet on the Páramo of Antisana

Montane forest leaves

Montane forest with
giant ferns on a lava
cliff below Reventador
volcano

OVERLEAF
The San Rafael Falls
on the Coca river

remaining Indians, or driving them before them away from the larger streams. The best species of rubber-yielding *Hevea* trees grew on the upper southern tributaries, the Juruá, Purús and Madeira, where the rains allowed collection for only six months of the year. In order to get the maximum return of rubber˙ the trees were often simply cut down and the sap collected from the fallen trunk with no thought to the future. The fortunes made by the traders, who supplied food and Winchester rifles to the rubber-tappers at exorbitant prices, resulted in the boom of Manaus and the construction of its famous opera-house, opened in 1896.

Although demand soared no rubber trees were planted, and increased supply meant more and more men working deeper into the jungle. But in 1876 Sir Henry Wickham had sailed from the Tapajós with a cargo of 70,000 seeds destined for the Royal Botanic Gardens at Kew. Only 4% germinated, but they were the beginning of plantations in Ceylon and Malaya which put plantation rubber on the market in 1912. When World War 1 broke out two years later the boom collapsed, and the tide of penniless fever-stricken *seringueiros* ebbed back out of the forest.

The exploitation mentality still continues. In Peru hardwoods are felled by roving timber-cutters with chain-saws, who shape the timber on the spot into railway sleepers which they drag single-handed to the rivers and float to the roadhead. In the state of Pará in Brazil the giant massaranduba trees are felled rather than tapped for their latex, which is used in the plastics industry.

The traditional slash-and-burn agriculture involved cutting and burning a small area of forest, planting manioc, rice, beans and bananas in the ashes, and allowing the crop to grow up through the tangle of felled tree-trunks. Only two or at most three harvests are possible before the nutrients in the ashes are used up. The plot is then left to be slowly recolonised by secondary growth species and finally the forest itself. If large areas are burnt, not only will many of the nutrients in the ash wash off the surface with the rainfall and be lost into the rivers, but there will be very slow regeneration from the surrounding forest.

Early attempts at colonisation on a large scale by burning and cultivating forested areas failed due to the unsuitability of the infertile and fragile forest soils. Such was the fate of the Bragantina area east of the port of Belém, cleared at the turn of the century, and even provided with a railway to encourage settlement by colonists from Spain, Portugal, and France. Over 10,000 square miles were reduced to a stunted scrub 'ghost landscape' in less than fifty years. The water-holding capacity of the soil has been upset and the droughts are longer, due to the large bare areas of soil which erode rapidly into the rivers.˙

A very similar mistake was made by the Brazilian government when it encouraged burning the forest for cattle ranching. This was done on an enormous scale in the '60's and early '70's when tax concessions were given to major European and American companies to 'develop' Amazonia. For example Volkswagen de Brasil was reported as burning 120,000 hectares for ranching. In practise the good grass which grows initially is taken over within a few years by inedible woody species, which it is too costly to remove, and the pasture quickly degenerates. The profitability of such areas depends entirely on the unreal world of accountancy, of tax holidays and inflation, while the real value of the land is lost. Yet the governments of Brazil and Peru still view Amazonia as a resource to be developed.

A new era in the history of the Amazon began on 6 June 1970 when President Médici of Brazil visited the north-east of his country during the worst drought experienced there in thirty years. In a moving speech the President promised to take immediate action. Ten days later the National Integration Programme was created, setting in motion the immediate construction of the Transamazonican highway and the Cuiabá-Santarem highway, the first of fourteen major highways. The Transamazonica, leading west to Benjamin Constant on the Peruvian frontier, is longer than New York to San Francisco.

The plan was to shift five million of the starving population from the north-east of Brazil to agricultural settlements replacing the forest. The details were hurriedly drawn up without any of the cost-benefit analysis customary before such massive investment, and they now seem incredibly naive. Every ten kilometres along the Transamazonica an Agrovilla would be set up with 48–64 houses, each with a 100 hectare plot, an elementary school, an ecumenical chapel, a small store, a pharmacy and a clinic. Every fifty kilometres there would be an Agropolis of up to 500 houses, a high-school, a brickworks, saw-mill, gas-station, etc. Every 150 kilometres a Ruropolis, an agricultural development centre serving a population of 50,000. The colonist had to feed himself from the beginning with little or no starting capital.

Colonists who had set themselves up along the banks of the Amazon earlier tended to be those who were unable to cope within the cities, 'marginated' by the demands of a society with which they were unable to compete because of lack of education or intelligence. To survive on the new roads was a hard task even if the ground was fertile, and most of it was not. The roads were pushed through without any regard to the Indian population whose lands were protected by the Brazilian Constitution.

The roads are still being built, for political rather than economic reasons, but everywhere they herald the destruction of more forest. The settlement scheme is generally considered to have been a disaster, and has officially been stopped. Schemes which sold land to foreign companies such as the Italian Liquigás for less than a penny an acre are things of the past, and there is an increasingly powerful environmental lobby in Brazil itself. But with the appalling poverty in Brazil's great cities and in the north-east, with Brazil's continuing balance of payments problems, and its shortage of petroleum, pressure remains to seek economic development of the 'untouched resources' of Amazonia.

Two notable attempts have been made to dispel the belief that it is impossible to obtain a continuous productive return from rain-forest soils. In 1926 Henry Ford began a scheme of rubber plantations on the Tapajós. Nearly three million trees were planted, but fungus disease was such a problem that the project was never economic. Then in 1967, Daniel K. Ludwig, the American inventor of the super-tanker, bought four million acres of Amazonian forest for 75 cents an acre at Jari. He then spent a billion dollars developing rice-fields, a china-clay mine, and plantations for a paper-pulp mill which he had floated in from Japan. It was a massive gamble, and despite the fact that the mill is producing a hundred million dollars-worth of pulp a year, it will never return Ludwig's original investment. The costs were too high and the production of timber is too low. Rice yields are also thirty percent below target.

But the whole massive Jari project went ahead without one crucial piece of evidence. Nobody knows whether it is possible to take repeated crops of trees from the Amazonian soils without successively depleting them. (It is impracticable to provide artificial fertiliser.) The answer will not be known until the 1990's, and if crops of trees cannot be sustained it will exert a powerful influence on the future of the rain-forest.

Two arguments against the felling of tropical forest that have been used with some emotion have to be viewed with care.

Reports have been widely circulated that the Amazon forest is the lung of the world, and that cutting it down would deprive the atmosphere of half its oxygen supply. About 0.05% of the world's oxygen supply is produced each year from plants by photosynthesis, and even if 50% did come from the Amazon, it is likely that most of what is produced is reabsorbed by the fungi breaking down leaf litter. It is certain that we have not heard the end of this story but it illustrates the danger of making sweeping statements about the forest.

More serious is the charge that burning the forest would release such high levels of carbon-dioxide into the atmosphere that the air would warm up, melting ice-caps, and raising the level of the sea. If all the Amazon forest were to be burnt it has been calculated that this would increase atmospheric CO_2 by 10%. It is thought that the percentage has already been increased by 15% in the last hundred years by burning fossil fuel. On balance it may be that burning fossil fuel is more significant and potentially detrimental to our climate than burning forests.

The publicity given to the destruction of Amazonia has tended to obscure the fact that since 1975 conservation areas totalling 10,000 square kilometres have been set aside, doubling the area of the American tropics under conservation, and covering roughly half of the forest refuges. More reserves are needed and much is still to be done to control exploitation within them, but it is a very encouraging start.

It is said that D.K. Ludwig made his fortune by sitting at his desk thinking four to five years ahead. The Indian tribes seen by Orellana had thought in terms of their children and their tribes' future and had a way of life which the forest could sustain for ever. It seems that modern governments lack both the will and the ability to acquire this sort of perspective.

11

Filming the Amazon Rain-Forest

In the starlight the sharp black ridges of the Andes fell away to the east from a void beneath us. At five in the morning we knelt in frozen ichu grass on the edge of the known world, where the Incas had worshipped the rising sun. Slowly sky and earth divided with a paling and a yellowing and suddenly the immensity of the rain forest spread twelve thousand feet below, its secrets hidden in a dark sea of leaves and mist. Far away, further than seemed possible, a yellow spark shone and doubled and glared, and in a few seconds more the peaks of the Cordillera Vilcabamba behind us blazed sunlit white against the dark high-altitude sky.

For a few instants the sun staggered in its vertical ascent, trembled, and even sank earthwards, its colour changing to blue; then it tore itself free of the refracting layers above the forest and climbed over the last great wilderness on earth. Frost glittered on the moss and alpine blooms about us, and from the valleys layers of cloud coalesced to shield bromeliads and orchids from the day. Now we were to travel down, to sink beneath those clouds so far below, along a single-track switchback road with hairpin bends inside tunnels, abandoning our condor's-eye-view.

We were en route for the Amazon lowland rain forest, the Manu park, named after a tributary of the Madre de Dios, itself a tributary of the Madeira, which joins the Amazon below Manaus. With me were Donaldo and Neil Rettig, a cameraman from Chicago with a wide experience of filming in the jungle who had the invaluable ability to climb trees using tree-surgeon's spikes. By then we already had considerable experience of the difficulties of filming in the jungle, where we had spent the last seven weeks.

Our most accessible location had been the Explorers Inn on the Tambopata river near the Bolivian frontier in Peru. A tourist lodge, it incorporates a reserve of about 5000 hectares of lowland forest somewhat drier than that found nearer the Amazon proper. It is famous amongst specialists in South American birds for having the largest number of species (511 when we were there) of any five square kilometre area in the continent. This means that it has more bird species than anywhere else in the world, and they range from the monkey-eating Harpy Eagle to tiny humming-birds.

There are many tourist lodges in Amazonia, especially around Iquitos where they are mostly set in forest that has long since had its hardwoods removed, and is often secondary growth. Most of the animals were shot for the pot or for export years ago, and although some are returning since the export of live animals from Peru was banned in 1974, Iquitos is a poor place to get an idea of the jungle. The headwaters of the Tambopata, however, are still occupied by Indian tribes who successfully resisted earlier incursions into the forest by timber extractors, and now a considerable gold-rush on the neighbouring Madre de Dios is deflecting pressure of colonisation. For several years Max Gunther has had the enlightened policy of encouraging scientists to stay at the Explorers Inn while studying the forest, and the result is that it is the best inventoried area in western Amazonia. It is found that from twenty to fifty percent of the species collected are unknown to science!

Along the banks of most rivers the forest appears as an exuberant growth of trees great and small, thickly hung with vines and lianas. In less frequented areas there will be many kingfishers, herons, and storks, and from time to time troops of monkeys, and the basket nests of oropendolas hanging from trees. Paddling a canoe, or even travelling in a speedboat – a popular method on the Amazon – is an agreeable experience, at least for the first few hours.

Inside the forest everything is different. The first surprise is that it is so open. Few tropical forests approach the popular idea of 'jungle', and in fact we never worked in any Amazonian area that was as hard to get through as the bamboo forest of Chiloé in south Chile. But it is dark, and cool, and drab. It is very difficult to take a photograph of the inside of the forest that looks interesting because there appears to be no form to it and there is either not enough light, or in patches too much. The ground is scattered with a thin layer of dead leaves, some of them of enormous size, from which grow saplings, herbaceous plants and small trees. Above these stand the thin straight whitish trunks of the trees of the lower canopy. Compared to the forests of Tierra del Fuego, there is hardly any fallen timber and compared to the montane forest, there are few mosses and epiphytes growing on the trees, though one does catch sight of leaf-forms surprisingly familiar from hotel lobbies. Here and there a huge trunk will be supported by great web-like buttresses, perhaps with roots curling across the ground like huge snakes. Others have conical clusters of spiked prop-roots joining the stem at head-height above the ground. Lianas hang in loops and tangles from the canopy, through which the biggest trees tower to stand in the full sunlight. The overwhelming impression is of silence and emptiness. Both of these are illusions: the forest is not silent at all, but it absorbs sound to such an extent that it is quite useless to scream for help if you are lost. Nor is it empty, though the amount of animal life compared to the quantity of vegetable growth is very small.

It is not an easy place to work owing to the humidity and the insects, but however unpleasant it may be carrying a heavy load down a trail, dodging lianas which hook at one's back-pack, stumbling in holes where trees have ceased to exist, and catching a face-full of spiders' webs, stop for an instant, stretch one's senses and something never fails to astound. The colour that glints in a butterfly, or its mimicry of fallen leaves, the brilliance of a tanager, the shape of an insect or the industry of ants. Here was a huge solitary ant (*paraponera*), an inch long. Neil had once been bitten by one as he climbed down a tree. He said he thought he was going to die with the pain, and the fever which it gave him lasted three days. But this one was behaving strangely, running and hiding under leaves. It was being pursued by a parasitic phorid fly that was trying to lay an egg on the back of the ant's neck. If it succeeded the egg would hatch to form a maggot which would eat the ant alive.

As Darwin wrote: 'In England any person fond of natural history enjoys in his walks a great advantage, by always having something to attract his attention; but in these fertile climates teeming with life the attractions are so numerous that he is scarcely able to walk at all.'

Except on the river's edge the forest is not a place of beautiful open vistas, and one has to learn to look for the detail: the mannakin dancing to its female in a thicket, the ants' nest, hidden under the curl of a leaf, whose warriors rush out and drum a rattling tattoo on the leaf at the threat of any disturbance. The pleasure that observing the jungle brings is more often intellectual than aesthetic. But it is one thing to stand still and have the luck to see an ocelot creep past, it is quite another to go out in search of a particular creature. Even the noisiest of birds, like the screaming piha, can be remarkably difficult to see through the intervening screen of tree-trunks and lianas. For example, although we were able to record the extraordinary melody of the musician wren several times, we never managed to film it.

There are, of course, mammals that live on the forest floor, like red brocket deer and wild pigs – the white-lipped peccary can even form very dangerous large herds. Ancient animals like the armadilloes anteaters and even bush dogs roam there, but many of the larger animals live in the trees or rivers. For thousands of years the combination of deep floods and meagre vegetation on the ground have driven animals to adapt to an arboreal way of life. The prehensile tail is only found in the forests of the Americas, yet it occurs on such widely different groups of animals as the monkey (primate), kinkajou (carnivore), porcupine (rodent), and tamandua anteater (edentate). A fifth grasping limb is a useful appendage when eating in trees!

The usual way to observe what is going on in the canopy is either to cut the tree down, or to build a metal tower. The first method would be laughable if it was not done so often; the second brings terrible limitations of time and cost. To my knowledge there are only two permanent towers in the whole of Amazonia, so they are restricting to say the least. This was why Neil's ability to climb trees and build filming platforms was so important.

His technique in Peru was to hunt for a tree that was in flower or fruiting and attracting the attention of birds and monkeys. He would then chose a tree nearby which had a triple crotch at about the right height for a triangular platform. Donaldo would cut saplings and haul them up with a pulley, and Neil would tie them in place with cord, decking the structure with thinner saplings.

He and Donaldo could build one of these and get the camera into action in three hours. It was, however, by no means always straightforward.

The tree selected would frequently be covered with lianas which had to be cleared as it was climbed, and these could conceal wasps' or bees' nests, not to mention the ants. On one occasion Neil had climbed a fine big tree with the necessary open canopy well above the surrounding trees. He was just about to get Donaldo to haul up the poles when he realised that the big limb he was standing on was completely rotten from termites, and liable to drop off at any moment. He was half way up the next tree when a huge cloud of small bees started stinging him – the usual stingless sweat bees just climbed into his hair and continuously round his eyes and into his mouth and nose. At the same time he saw some macaws feeding in another tree, which was, as he put it, 'a good excuse to come down.' But in the meantime the rope that was attached to his waist, down which he had to slide, had become entangled in the vicious barbs of a climbing bamboo.

Donaldo, while trying to free the rope, became enveloped in a cloud of white dust shaken from the bamboo which stung his skin painfully wherever it made contact. Neil was shouting to him to hurry up so that he could get clear of the bees and Donaldo could only reply 'I'm covered in this stinging dust.' They managed to get Neil down in safety but it was not until Neil got some of the dust on his own arm that he realised what the problem was. Donaldo tore his shirt off and in his own words 'was running blind round the forest crashing into trees like a wounded tapir.' It was extremely painful all that night, and someone gave him a couple of anti-histamine pills. He afterwards complained that he spent the night 'sleeping on the ceiling.' We knew that bamboo dust could be irritant, but none of us had any idea it could be like that. As Donaldo put it: 'There are too many things in this forest that I don't want to know about.'

On another occasion Donaldo was walking through the forest recording birds, watching the canopy rather than where he was putting his feet. He heard a faint rattle on the leaves and looked down to see a seven-foot-long bushmaster snake sliding across the track one pace away. Luckily he was walking slowly. The bushmaster is one of the largest, and by far the deadliest, of the snakes in the forest. It injects so much poison, being so big, that even if you have anti-serum it probably will not save your life.

Another tree which we got to know well was the tangarana or triplaris, also called the *palo santo* (holy tree) or greenhorn tree. This is a smallish tree which is quite common in flood-plain areas with very pretty flowers which are used ornamentally. It is a good example of the extraordinary relationships so prevalent in the forest. To outward appearances there is nothing odd about the tree, but if one taps the segmented trunk large ants with a poisonous bite come scurrying out of special holes and swarm all over the tree and the surrounding ground. The trunk of the tree has a small circular channel down its centre which connects to tunnels in all the branches and even twigs, so that ants can run up the centre of the trunk and right out to the base of the leaves themselves to defend them against herbivores – insects or mammals. These Azteca ants have a most painful bite with a sort of delayed reaction, so that three or four can get their mandibles well into your skin before the burning starts. They also nip off the tips of lianas or other plants trying to grow near their tree which might compete for nutrients in the soil. It is because the nutrients are so scarce that trees cannot afford to lose many leaves to herbivores, so some fill their leaves with toxic substances (many of which are important for human medicine, such as quinine, curare, etc.). Others have invested in ants. Without the ants they cannot survive, and in return the tree provides lodging. Another shrub, the tococa, provides little twin-roomed chambers at the base of each leaf which contains families of tiny ants ready to defend their pastures against insects.

I was anxious to see what kind of material Neil was getting, and I got him to pull up a mountaineering rope and fasten it to the platform. I had had a lesson in how to use a sit-harness and jumars, clamps that slide up a rope so that you can climb it using the power of a leg, but here I was very much on my own and I had to clear the ground with a machete before I could get under the platform. The rope stretched a lot and I bounced, wondering whether I had connected the equipment the right way round, and slowly worked my way up until I got into the first tangle of branches. I then had to draw a very sharp knife to cut them. It was not a nice feeling to be chopping away with both hands free near the rope that held me thirty feet up. Slowly I worked my way higher. Now there was another problem: the rope had been up all night and the ants had found it and begun to use it as a short cut to the top of the tree. Every time I slid up a jumar, another twenty would drop onto me and several more would go down my neck. Fortunately they did not bite as badly as the Azteca. There was no going back as I would have found it just as hard work going down again. In the end I made it to the top, after scaring myself almost rigid, and eased myself onto the platform. Here it was a different world of brilliant light and flowers and the huge green intersecting domes of tree crowns. Clouds towered into the sky and macaws and parrots flew past squawking. On the branches a lizard hunted the ants that had been hunting me. It probably never ventured onto the ground. Humming-birds dipped at the blossoms and the tree stirred gently in the breeze. Looking back down my rope into the gloom beneath I saw a heliconid butterfly perch on it, attracted by its bright colour. Below were the sombre shadows where I always had the feeling that the forest was waiting for me to make one false step. I appreciated why Neil had to surround himself with pieces of towel soaked in insecticide to try to keep down the population of sweat bees. They were appalling.

There were many brazil-nut trees at the Explorers Inn. We could see the hard dark-brown cannon-ball-like pods hanging far above the canopy. They are one of the most dangerous things in the jungle, because they are heavy and fall with such force that they will break branches off trees and kill a man unfortunate enough to get a direct hit. The tough shell is the result of an evolutionary battle with the macaw which eats the nuts. Over the ages the pod of the nut and the beak of the macaw have been growing steadily tougher. I once watched a group of pet macaws eating what I took to be dog-biscuits. They were holding pieces in their clawed feet and crunching them with their beaks. Then I realised that they were actually crunching up bricks! They work round the nut like a tin-opener, and although they still succeed in breaking the shell, its toughness slows the feeding rate and makes the macaw spend more energy, deflecting it onto other easier meat.

Another animal which has a fondness for brazil nuts is the agouti. It is enough to thump the ground in the forest like a falling nut to attract them. They gnaw open the woody pods, and then carry off the nuts, which are of course the seeds of the tree, and bury them. This is of great advantage to the tree because any sapling growing up near the parent tree will be in its shade, and may also be attacked by any diseases or herbivores damaging the parent. It happens that the agouti chooses soft soil to bury the nut, which is ideal for the nut to germinate in, provided the agouti does not find it again and eat it. In practice agoutis find less than a third of the nuts they bury.

Brazil nuts are so valuable as a forest product that in Brazil it is illegal to cut the trees down. Consequently lone brazil-nut trees are frequently left standing when the forest is destroyed. This reveals a complete lack of understanding of the intricacy of the forest ecology. The tree is pollinated by bees, but the flower has a spring-loaded defense to protect its pollen. Only the heaviest forest bumble-bees can open it. But the brazil-nut is a seasonal tree and for eleven months of the year the bee must feed elsewhere. Cut the forest and you have no bees, and no nuts.

From the air the River Ucayali loops and doubles in the most extraordinary fashion across the green expanse of the forest. It is one of the great tributaries which, when it joins the River Marañón, forms the Amazon proper. It is also one of the most tangled tributaries, not just one river but a whole ravelled skein of loops and ox-bow lakes, islands and canals. Over 2500 miles from the Atlantic it is still only 500 feet above the sea, and in the rainy season it rises by up to thirty feet. The river Tambopata had been near enough the Andes to retain some speed of flow, and the Explorers Inn stood at 850 feet, with a much more pronounced dry season. Now we were flying over the great wet sponge that lies in the lowlands of the Amazon basin. It seems hardly possible that this saturated area should have dried out during the last ice-age while the forest on the Tambopata remained, but the evidence is that this was the case, which accounts for the richness of bird and insect species there.

We were in a Pilatus float-plane heading for a solitary house on the bank of the river Pacaya which gives its name to the Pacaya Samiria National Reserve, five thousand square miles of forest, 130 miles south-west of Iquitos as the plane flies. Hardly anybody has heard of the reserve, let alone visited it, and a float plane had never been landed on the river before.

It was a relief to find the hut in that tangle of rivers and lagoons, identifiable because it had the ten-ton canoe moored alongside which I had sent off with our supplies four days before. I had used those valuable four days to film elsewhere. I was also relieved to see that the boatmen had found their way, as Cahuana is a long way from the nearest village. We splashed down without incident, and with some difficulty turned round in the narrow river and taxied back to the hut. Pink inias and grey dolphins huffed and dived around us as we ran gently up onto the shore.

Pekka Soini, the Finnish biologist with whom we had come to stay, had paddled across the river in a tiny dug-out canoe. As he hardly ever visits Iquitos he is a hard man to contact and this was the first time I had met him. He looked the archetype of a man who has spent his life in the tropics, incredibly gaunt, with hollow cheeks, a pointed chin and a thin reddish beard. He was once the local manager in Iquitos for Cruceiro, the Brazilian airline, with a wife and two children and the comfortable life-style of a prosperous businessman. Ten years ago he left everything behind and went to live full-time in the jungle. Sharing his exile, and the only other inhabitant of Cahuana was Maria, a petite Argentinian girl with earnest eyes hidden behind enormous dark glasses, a broad face, and a torrent of dark hair to her waist. Despite our thirty crates of food and equipment piled on their verandah they both seemed delighted to see us, and we were soon sharing a big jug of cool river-water and fresh fruit-juice. It was the first of many acts of selfless hospitality that Maria showered on us when we came in at all hours of the day, tired, hungry, wet through with sweat or rain, and usually filthy.

The house was set on a point where the river had broken through the neck of an ox-bow lagoon. Now the river was about twelve metres below, but at the time of the floods in April it flowed right under the floor. Like all local houses it was built on stilts. Now we heard that Pekka had had an extraordinarily bad piece of luck, yet one indicative of the difficulties of doing research in Peru. He had taken his first leave in several years and had been away from the house for two months. During that time fishermen, who had no right to be in the reserve, camped at the house and stole everything that was moveable and even took the floor and the mosquito screens forming the walls. He arrived back to a derelict ruin. That had been only six weeks before our arrival. A carpenter was still putting up the new screens on the living room and we were able to give a little help to the finishing touches. Although Pekka had fortunately taken most of his books and valuables with him, the worst part was that the fishermen appeared to have shot the troupe of friendly woolly monkeys, and the family of capybaras that Pekka had been studying, and had scared off many of the other animals habituated to his presence which we had come to film. It was a bitter blow both for him and us.

The hut only had two rooms, so we pitched two tents on the verandah to sleep in. Fortunately they had mosquito-nets. There were quite a few mosquitoes about in the jungle during the day, but sharp at 6.0 p.m. when it got dark they came out in hordes the like of which I had never experienced. Pekka said that they were worse in the rainy season, but it was difficult to believe it. The air was filled with their thin whine and they dropped to the attack half-dozens at a time. It was impossible to stand still for a moment without being

139

covered in them. We retreated into the screened study-cum-dining-room, and began to discuss our tactics. Pekka explained that he was working on a census of animals on the island inside the old loop of the river opposite the house, and also on turtles and capybaras.

Capybaras are the largest rodents, looking like something between a guinea-pig and a hippopotamus. They grow to one metre, 20 cms long and are half a metre high at the shoulders. Though they also graze on land, they spend a great deal of time in the water where they have a formidable enemy, the anaconda.

On my first visit to the Explorers Inn, I was travelling the fifty miles from Puerto Maldonado upstream to the Inn in a small canoe with two boatmen when the connecting-rod on the engine broke (due to lack of oil in the sump!) and we began to drift back down the river. I have long since learned to be philosophical when things go wrong in South America, and although it was soon pitch dark, it was dry and there were few insects, so I was quite enjoying drifting silently with the current past the noises of the jungle night. The crew, however, began to get agitated, and when I asked why, they said they were afraid of anacondas.

Colonel Fawcett's account of anacondas is well known: 'I sprang for my rifle as the creature began to make its way up the bank, and hardly waiting to aim smashed a .44 soft-nosed bullet into its spine, ten feet below the wicked head. At once there was a flurry of foam, and several heavy thumps against the boat's keel, shaking us as though we had run on a snag.

'With great difficulty I persuaded the Indian crew to turn in shorewards. They were so frightened that the whites showed all round their popping eyes, and in the moment of firing I had heard their terrified voices begging me not to shoot lest the monster destroy the boat and kill everyone on board, for not only do these creatures attack boats when injured, but also there is great danger from their mates.

'We stepped ashore and approached the reptile with caution – it was out of action, but shivers ran up and down the body like puffs of wind on a mountain tarn. As far as it was possible to measure, a length of forty-five feet lay out of the water, and seventeen feet in it, making a total length of sixty-two feet.'

But the New York Zoological Society has offered a reward of $5000 since the turn of the century for any snake over thirty feet in length. This has never been claimed and is still on offer. I took the attitude that most stories about anacondas were gross exaggerations.

At Cahuana, Pekka told us a story which rather changed my views. One night Pekka and Maria had both been in small canoes doing a night census of the capybaras only a hundred yards from the house. There was one about to drink from the river, about two-thirds full size, and weighing perhaps thirty kilos. It was only about three metres from their canoes, staring at the water in front of it. 'Then between us and the capybara a big anaconda lunged out of the water and grabbed the capybara by the nose. Quicker than you could snap your fingers it had thrown coils around it and had dragged it into the water out of sight,' said Pekka. 'There was no time to tell it to stop!' He laughed. 'And that capybara was bigger than Maria if she had been bending down at the water.'

'Make sure you have water in your tents at night,' said Maria. 'It's dangerous to go down to the river, their heads are so small that you don't see them.'

We did not need to be told twice.

Anacondas are aquatic boas, and are mostly nocturnal, lying up in the forest or in shallows during the day. They are fast swimmers, but will often drift downstream showing only their heads above water. They eat fish, but also animals, which are usually caught as they come down to drink. There are plenty of reports of them fighting caimans, South American alligators. There are also a number of authentic reports of people being bitten by them. The snake's technique is to bite and then throw coils round the prey, passing them over its own head so that there is no need to wind round and round. The prey is then dragged into the water and drowned. It seems very likely that children at least must be caught by anacondas. They are known to catch domestic animals, and children living in the jungle spend half their time in the rivers.

Pekka used to swim in the river at Cahuana, but after seeing the anaconda he stopped. Also the fishermen had gutted and dried fish at the house, making a great mess of fish remains, and Pekka no longer trusted the piranhas. There was also a ten-foot-long white caiman called Tomás. Once when they had had nothing but rice to eat for ten days Tomás had caught a huge fish and in shaking it in his jaws had thrown a piece weighing about six pounds up into the forest. Pekka later found it and it made a welcome change of diet.

A couple of days later Neil was up a platform and Donaldo was recording, and I wanted to make another platform on a fallen tree which lay stretched out in the lagoon. I paddled off in one of the tiny dug-out canoes. These were round-bottomed except for a little keel aft, and felt horribly unstable. They are paddled from the bow, and I set off gingerly dipping my paddle from side to side. No anacondas were visible, but if I dropped a piece of mud into the water it was at once attacked from all sides by piranhas.

It was a perfect tropical morning with cumulus clouds towering above the tall liana-hung trees on either hand. The black water of the lagoon, or cocha, was so calm that it seemed the prow was parting the sky, so clear were the reflections of the clouds below it. Amazon kingfishers hovered in the air and dived, anhingas with their long cormorant-like necks plopped suddenly into the water to hide. Hoatzins fluttered clumsily from branch to branch, while great horned screamers and several kinds of birds of prey, including one that was diving to catch fish, watched my silent progress. A group of squirrel-monkeys, one of the prettiest kinds, squeaked and twittered in a fruiting tree, leaping with a crash from branch to branch.

Suddenly the water boiled beside me, the canoe lurched, and I struggled to keep it upright. Then silence again. The water told me nothing but I felt profoundly shocked. It must have been an *Arapaima gigas*, the paiche or giant redfish, one of the largest freshwater fish in the world frequently reaching over two metres in length and over 90 kilos in weight. There were plenty at

Cahuana, but it is one of the few places in the Amazon where they survive in any number, so much is their flesh prized.

The cocha at Cahuana was still connected to the Pacaya at one end, but it had little opportunity to flow except during the flood season. Consequently it was filled with black water from the forest. To help cope with the lack of oxygen in the cochas, which are frequently separated from the river systems for most of the year, the Arapaima has a large swim-bladder connected to its gullet which it uses as a lung. Its family can be traced back over 100 million years, and its lung demonstrates one of the features which had to evolve before the amphibians could climb from water onto land for the first time.

It has been estimated that there are about two thousand different species of fish in the Amazon, and since World War II there has been an enormous trade, from cities like Iquitos, Manaus, and Leticia, in the more brightly coloured small fish for aquaria. What is not appreciated, however, is how important the fish are to the life of the forest and vice versa. They form part of the complex web of interactions which is so little understood.

Until recently caimans were shot in large numbers for their skins, or to make hideous mounted toys for tourists. Caimans eat fish, but far from the numbers of fish increasing, they actually went down with the loss of the caimans. This was because the caimans ate fish which migrated during the flood season from the white water rivers into the cochas where they spawned. The faeces of the caimans added valuable salts to the water which fed plankton in turn eaten by the young fish.

Because there is so little light in the rivers there is very little primary production of plankton, etc., and the life of the waters relies greatly on leaves, fruit and insects dropping in from the forest. Many fish eat fruit from the trees. Indeed it is claimed that the electric fish, which packs 350 volts, shakes down the fruit of the assaí palm with its electric shock. It was startling how quickly a fruit dropped into the river would be snapped up, as if fish were already waiting with open jaws. Since they eat fruit and can also migrate up to 300 miles, fish are very important agents for spreading seeds that pass through their gut into the forest, especially during the periods when the water is high and they actually swim between the trees.

There are many families of predatory fish in Amazon waters. Most of them, like the paiche, feed on other fish, but of all of them the most famous is the piranha. Six of the twenty-five Amazonian species eat seeds, but they probably all eat other fish, some having mouths adapted to strip scales, others fins. They have extremely powerful jaws and head-bones, and their interlocking triangular teeth are so sharp that they can bite through almost any living substance, including bone. The dangerous species in the Amazon and Orinoco is *Serrasalmus nattereri* which is eight to ten inches long and takes a bite about the size of a nutmeg. The teeth are so sharp that the bite cuts away the flesh instantly, and of course they attack in shoals. There is no doubt that in certain rivers, especially when they are concentrated by the dry season, these red-bellied piranha can be very dangerous. But I have struggled in rapids hauling canoes in areas where I have also caught and eaten piranha, and few people who work in the rain forest have not swum in cochas that abound with them. Like sharks they appear to be attracted by blood or a commotion on the surface. They are also dangerous when caught, being easily capable of biting through a shoe and the foot inside it.

Another dangerous fish which attacks in shoals, and annually accounts for the lives of fishermen on the cataracts of the river Madeira, is the whale candirú of the family Cetopsidae. It should not be confused with the other unrelated candirú, a tiny fish which parasitises the gill chambers of fish and has the revolting habit of swimming up the anus or vagina of bathers. It is very difficult to remove as it has backwards-facing spines.

But of all these fish the local people most fear the sting ray which lies on the sand-banks. It is very easy to step on, when it inflicts an extremely painful wound with a poisoned barb on its tail, a wound which frequently does not heal without recourse to antibiotics.

Although the Pacaya was in theory a white-water river, we had seen how its cochas – the old ox-bow lakes of the flood plain – tended to be black-water, except during the flood season, and indeed the distribution of soils is extremely complex on a small scale. It is extraordinary to find clay soils which have aluminium and iron but almost no silica, next to white sands which have almost nothing but silica. The high forest grew on the raised land which was not flooded, but even this land was not inviolate by the rivers, because in their constant serpentine scouring they eroded out their bends, cutting cliffs into the soft sedimentary soil, toppling the forest giants on one side and leaving low sand-banks covered with secondary growth of cane and secropia on the other. Within the forest itself the presence or absence of swampy lowlands can have a marked effect on the vegetation.

It was Pekka Soini who first noticed how two species of titi-monkey, although living in the same general area of forest, actually used different habitats. One species kept to the higher terrain and the other preferred the river banks, though both of them ate fruit 70 percent of the time. On the Nanay river we visited Mishana, where Warren Kinsey has been studying the yellow-handed titi-monkey since 1974. He has found that it is almost exclusively restricted to white-sand areas of forest, while its relative, the dusky titi, at times surrounds it on clay soils where it eats leaves as well as fruit. The white-sand vegetation has a lower rate of production of leaves and fruits than that of the better clay soils and fruits are smaller, so the yellow-handed titi has developed a different supplement, eating insects which are more numerous there.

It is likely that the yellow-handed titi developed during one of the dry periods of the Amazon when it was separated from most of its fellows on a white-sand forest refuge near the Rio Negro. It is fascinating that each subspecies of titi-monkey is distributed near a probable refuge area, a small example of how the complexity of species in the jungle has been built up.

We were filming the titis one day at Mishana, when suddenly the young monkey, feeding near its parents, just let go of a branch and crashed thirty feet to the jungle floor. In six years of observation Warren Kinsey had never seen anything like it happen before and he was most puzzled. The monkey was unhurt and went on feeding. A little later we heard an extraordinary noise of rushing in the air. We speculated whether it might have been a meteorite as it was so loud, but in the evening we saw a pair of king vultures perched in their black and white finery on a tree protruding above the canopy. Later we got evidence that it was they that had frightened the monkey, and it was the sound of one stooping that had been so impressive. It served to show how difficult it is to make sense of even dramatic occurrences in the forest.

Bats are extremely important members of the forest community: they pollinate trees, disperse seeds, and prey on a number of creatures. They make up no less than half the genera (families) of Amazonian animals yet they have hardly been studied at all. One bat, *Trichops cirrhosus*, can identify various frogs by the calls they produce, being able to chose between the poisonous and the edible ones which it hunts. Frogs call to attract mates and it is the mating call that also attracts the bat, but somehow the frogs have learned to detect the bat's presence and to stop calling and take evasive action if one appears. On the darkest nights they are not so good at keeping quiet, which makes it appear that they normally can see the bats, but there is also evidence that the bats shut off their sonar location device suggesting that the frogs can also hear them coming. What is interesting is that the poor frog pays a penalty for calling to potential mates. But the bat has to be careful, for if it attacks too large a kind of frog it may get eaten itself.

In temperate climates one of the main evolutionary forces is climatic stress. Animals have to survive winter as well as times of plenty in spring and summer. In the tropical forest animals and plants live in the relatively benign environment of a climate which fluctuates little (ice-ages apart). This allows great diversity as species can afford to become specialists in a particular food source, something that is impossible when food is seasonal. This in turn allows a great diversity of predators, and counter-predation strategies. The relationship between living organisms becomes the main force driving evolution and the relationships become ever more complex, a triumph of organisation of mutually dependant species, both a factory and a store of evolutionary diversity. That is what makes the forest so valuable and so hard to understand.

I had arranged with our boatman on the Manu that he provide food for himself and his four colleagues for two weeks, yet all he had brought was rice and a head of bananas. He intended to live off the land rather than spend money on stores, and we had none to spare. Just one or two professional hunters can cause terrible devastation among populations of the larger monkeys such as the spider monkey which only bears young every four years. It is always the bigger monkeys which are shot first for food even for road and oil-pipeline construction gangs. As we were in the buffer zone of the park I asked him not to shoot, expecting that he would fish instead. As it happened it was the nesting season for the river turtles, and instead he began to dig up their eggs.

144

In the nineteenth century turtles' eggs were so abundant that they were boiled down for oil for use in lamps. Bates described how 6000 jars of oil were exported each year from the upper Amazon to Belém. Each held three gallons, and he estimated that each harvest accounted for the destruction of forty-eight million eggs. Once, the Jesuits paid for their missions with this export. Now it is hard to find a beach in Amazonia where the turtles still breed. Yet it was useless to try to persuade our boatmen to leave any of the eggs behind.

Shintuya is the village at the end of the road from Cusco, where we had hired our canoes to reach the Manu river. It began as a mission, as did so many other Amazonian towns, in this case a Dominican mission to the Shintuya tribe. No outsider is allowed to own a house there, but that has not stopped the influence of outsiders. A Spanish Dominican priest was mowing the football pitch with a motor-mower when we arrived, and at some time past the Peruvian Navy had installed a huge quay with an enormous hangar-like shed for military equipment. I peered into its half-lit depths. The only thing it contained was a small pile of solidified sacks of cement. Outside lay a strange amphibious vehicle, their only vessel, bereft of its engine and surrounded by saplings growing up to hide it.

On the shore were piles of hardwood railway sleepers, each dragged from the steep jungle slopes by a sweating Indian with a chain-saw. They weighed 100 kilos (220 lbs). 'If you fall down they can kill you,' we were told. The missionaries controlled the trade.

There was also a large canoe full of empty beer-bottles from the gold miners on the Rio Colorado. The boatman was waiting for the lorry to arrive from Cusco with new supplies. He would have a long wait. The lorry had preceded us by a few hours on the road and I had seen the tracks from the double rear wheels leading over the edge of the precipice. For ten metres a track was cut slanting only a little down the slope. Then it stopped where the lorry had rolled. Far below was splintered woodwork and the bodies of the driver and his mate. Fifty Indians were scrambling over the mountainside hiding bottles of beer.

The saucy-eyed Indian women watched as we loaded our two boats deep into the water: our departure was the most exciting thing to happen for weeks. The river was raging after rain which had fallen all night, and huge trees were being swept past, roots and all. On the bank, oblivious to the world, stood a poor schizophrenic French girl. At least she was believed to be French, but she never spoke to anyone. The missionaries fed her. She was as thin as a lamp post, wearing a sleeveless tee-shirt and shorts, her limbs covered with insect bites which had turned into sores.

My last sight of 'civilisation' as we sped away from the bank on the boiling muddy water was of this girl staring into space making strange balletic movements with her arms and legs, absorbed in a private world. The Indian children watched her from afar and giggled. She carefully wiped the blackfly from her arms and legs and as quickly they settled again.

Four days later as we were chugging up the Manu river we saw a very crude

145

shelter on one of the beaches, a few palm fronds propped together. Three Indian women stood on the sand by the river-edge holding out jungle fruits towards us. They appeared to be of three different generations; a teen-age daughter, her mother and the grandmother perhaps. The oldest wore only a narrow cloth around her hips the other two wore tattered manufactured shirts and rudimentary skirts. They looked ugly and savage and desperate, no doubt exactly as the Indians of Tierra del Fuego had appeared to Darwin. They ran along the sand, holding out presents of fruit, imploring us to stop.

At the mouth of the Manu we had met two English botanists leaving the park, and they had told us about these Indian women. They were thought to be from a tribe that had never been contacted, since their language was different from both the Machigenga and the Amahuaca of the area. We are advised not to stop as it could be an ambush. Our boatmen were frightened, and I had only eight days left to film in the park without any other delays. I raised my hand and at once realised I was apeing a pale-face salute. The women began to get more and more agitated as they realised we were not going to stop. Tears ran down the younger one's face and as the second canoe with Neil and Donaldo went past she gestured, offering her body. I have never felt so ashamed of myself in my life. There was no doubt that *we* were the savages passing by on the other side.

The women had been there for two months, we discovered, when we arrived at the scientific post at Cocha Cashu. It was full of Americans studying monkeys, who did not appreciate the irony that there was an uncontacted tribe of their own kind only a few miles away.

The park guards had strict instructions not to contact the Indians, instructions which were not obeyed, hence the shirts and a machete that the women possessed. Those instructions, I was sure, were to avoid any awkward political involvement on the part of the Ministry of Agriculture in Lima, but they also implied the realisation that from the first handshake the tribe was doomed.

Was it not possible that we could work with them to save their forest? They were still there when we went back down the river a week later. One of them now wore a park ranger's hat, grabbed from his head and exchanged for a bead headband.

12

Epilogue

Picturesque names are not uncommon for towns in Amazonia. On the Ucayali stands Remate de Males (Culmination of evils), and on the way to The Explorer's Inn tourists are taken to an Indian village called Infierno (Hell). I accompanied one group being shown round by the ignorant boatman who treated the villagers much as one might treat animals in a zoo. He picked up their possessions and showed them to the tourists without any by-your-leave. He even picked up the little food they had, brazil-nuts and bananas, and handed it to the tourists. One immensely fat American woman was helping herself to armfuls of grapefruit knocked from a tree by the boatman. 'But here they have everything,' she exclaimed, walking off with her booty. The Indian family watched impassively from inside their hut. Nobody in the party even said 'Buenos Dias' to them.

The tourists were most offended when they caught sight of the villagers' prize possession, a small motor-cycle. It quite spoilt their idea of Paradise in Hell.

Most of Man's history has been spent trying to emancipate himself from the influence of the environment, and perhaps it is no accident that it is within the last quarter century, when the earth has been so dominated by man-made technology, when at least northern-hemisphere Man is often insulated from the effect of cold and famine, that the boom in outdoor pursuits such as sailing and bird-watching and adventure-holidays has really got under way. We have begun to realise that we need the natural world just as we have found the means finally to destroy it.

The destruction has been going on for a long time. Britain's oakwoods, the Caledonian Forest, the forests of Central Asia and the Altiplano, all have been burned generations ago, but the forecasts are frightening. Forty percent of the remaining forests in the less developed countries are expected to be felled before the end of the century. We British have already destroyed ours.

It was in 1922 that H.G. Wells wrote, 'Human history more and more becomes a race between education and catastrophe.' That was the year the BBC began broadcasting. In 1957 the year that London led the way with its clean air Act, one of the first effective anti-pollution measures, the BBC Television

Natural History Unit was formed. In countries as different as the Soviet Union, Britain, and Chile, animal programmes have a huge following. Only in the USA do 'creature features' have a bad name among TV executives. As they say themselves, 'birds don't sell.'

I believe that wildlife programmes do more than simply provide a new kind of circus. They really do engender an understanding of the world we are part of, and I can only hope that the scales will fall from the eyes of a journalist friend who felt I was wasting my time to spend two years filming the animals of the Andes. But if the message reaches the multinational corporations will it also reach Julio and Luis? Will they stop their cheerful predation on rare species? At least there seems little doubt that television will reach them.

Returning to a country after a twenty-year gap is bound to be an interesting experience, and not just to meet the beautiful daughters whom one had last seen as babes-in-arms. I remember in Chile in 1961 seeing a condor nailed to the outside of a Carabineros (police) post. This time I encountered a Carabineros post where they had confiscated a condor-chick from a Bolivian lorry-driver and were hand-rearing it to let it go free when it had grown. That's progress. So is the recovery in the populations of guanaco and vicuña. In Peru the huge Manu park is being preserved, in Ecuador they have had to limit the numbers of profitable visitors to the Galapagos islands for the sake of the disturbance to the wildlife. The idea that countries must live within the budget of their renewable resources is beginning to penetrate the political mind.

It was the heroic Villas Boas brothers, who worked so long to protect the Indians of the Xingu, who came to the conclusion that to prepare a tribe for integration was to prepare their destruction – because *we* are not sufficiently prepared.

The fact that there are still areas like the Manu containing large numbers of wild animals is owed entirely to the fact that they were defended by Indian tribes who viewed the animals as an essential part of their world and their culture. It would be to ignore history to believe that our more powerful civilisation will not in the end dominate theirs, but they have at least given us the chance to realise that the natural world is a part of our spiritual as well as our economic heritage.

I hope that *The Flight of the Condor* will not become simply an historical record of all that has been lost.

Bibliography

Bates, Henry Walter: *The Naturalist on the Amazons* (George Routledge and Sons, 1863)

Bridges, E. Lucas: *Uttermost Part of the Earth* (Hodder and Stoughton, 1951)

Darwin, Charles: *Journal of Researches during the voyage of HMS. Beagle* (Collins, 1860)

Dorst, Jean: *South America and Central America, a Natural History* (Hamish Hamilton, 1967)

Dourojeanni, Marc J. and Ponce, Carlos F.: *Los Parques Nacionales del Perú* (Incafo, Madrid, 1978)

Fittkau, E.J., etc. Editors: *Biogeography and Ecology in South America* Vols. 1, 2. (Junk, the Hague, 1968)

Francis, Peter: *Volcanoes* (Pelican, 1978)

Goodall, Rae Natalie Prosser: *Tierra del Fuego* (Ediciones Shanamaiim, Buenos Aires, 1979)

Goodland, R.J.A. and Irwin, H.S.: *Amazon Jungle: Green Hell to Red Desert* (Elsevier, 1975)

Goulding, Michael: *The Fishes and the Forest* (University of California Press, 1980)

Hudson, W.H.: *The Naturalist in La Plata* (Buenos Aires, 1892)

Janzen, Daniel H.: *Ecology of Plants in the Tropics* (Institute of Biology's Studies in Biology No. 58, Edward Arnold, 1975)

Johnson, A.W.: *The Birds of Chile* 2 vols and supplement (Platt, Buenos Aires, 1965)

Hemming, John: *The Conquest of the Incas* (Macmillan, 1970)

Hemming, John: *Red Gold* (Macmillan, 1978)

Keast, Allen, etc., Editors: *Evolution, Mammals and Southern Continents* (State University of New York Press, 1972)

Koford, Carl. B.: *The Vicuña and the Puna* (Ecological Monographs, Vol. 27, No. 2)

Murphy, R.C.: *The Oceanic Birds of South America* 2 vols (American Museum of Natural History, 1936)

Norton, I.O. and Sclater, J.G.: *A Model for the Evolution of the Indian Ocean and the Breakup of Gondwanaland* (Journal of Geophysical Research, Vol. 84, No. B12)

Schauensee, Rudolphe Meyer de: *A Guide to the Birds of South America* (Oliver and Boyd, 1971)

Schauensee, Rudolphe Meyer de: *A Guide to the Birds of Venezuela* (Princeton, 1978)

Shipton, Eric: *Tierra del Fuego: the Fatal Lodestone* (Charles Knight and Co. Ltd., 1973)

Snow, David W.: *The Web of Adaptation* (Collins, 1976)

Venegas, Claudio C.: *Guia de Campo para las Aves de Magallanes* (Monografia No. 11, Instituto de la Patagonia Chile, 1979)

Wallace, Alfred Russel: *Travels on the Amazon and Rio Negro* (Ward Lock and Co., 1889)

Whitmore, T.C., Editor: *Biogeography and Quaternary History in Tropical America* (Clarendon Press, Oxford, in prep.)

Whymper, Edward: *Travels amongst the Great Andes of the Equator* (Charles Knight and Co., 1972)

Picture Credits

The Flight of the Condor was produced by the Natural History Unit of the British Broadcasting Corporation and co-produced by WNET New York, from the BBC Bristol Network Production Centre.

Production Team

Series producer and writer	MICHAEL ANDREWS
Assistant producer	KEENAN SMART
Production assistants	JILLY BOOTH
	DONALDO MacIVER
Film cameramen	RODGER JACKMAN
	HUGH MILES
	NEIL RETTIG
	JIM SAUNDERS
	MARTIN SAUNDERS
	BRIAN SEWELL
Assistant cameramen	RED DENNER
	GEOFF PEARCE
Sound by	ROGER LONG
	DONALDO MacIVER
Film editors	PETER HEELEY
	TERESA HUGHES
Andean music performed by	ILLAPU
	INTI ILLIMANI
Chief scientific advisors	
Chile	OSCAR GONZALEZ
	LUIS PENA
	JURGEN ROTTMANN
Ecuador	JUAN BLACK
	PAUL GREENFIELD
Peru	PAUL DONAGHUE
	WARREN KINSEY
	GERARDO LAMAS
	AURELIO MALAGA
	PEKKA SOINI
Local organisers	JANET ANDREWS, SANTIAGO
	MARIE NEILSON, PUNTA ARENAS
	ELEANOR GRIFFIS, LIMA
	CARMEN MALAGA, IQUITOS
	MAURICIO DE ROMANA, AREQUIPA
	LIDA VON SCHEY, BUENOS AIRES

Index